Praise for Wh

This family memoir is a heartfelt, honest, often tongue-in-cheek view of life with an autistic child . . .

—LIBRARY JOURNAL

Parents of children with autism will find this book motivational as Mrs. Cariello focuses on the positive aspects of having a son with autism, while still including different struggles she and her family have gone through . . .

—NATIONAL ASSOCIATION OF SPECIAL EDUCATION TEACHERS

. . . a well-written testament that will undoubtedly help new parents of autistic children to cope with the news.

—CHICAGO CENTER FOR LITERATURE AND PHOTOGRAPHY

. . . a touching tribute to her family . . .

—PUBLISHERS WEEKLY

Every time I read something Carrie writes I am deeply moved. I laugh, I cry, I mourn with her and in the same breath feel equally encouraged.

—RACHEL HOLLIS, THE CHIC SITE

The chapters in *What Color is Monday?* reveal joy, heartbreak, hope, despair and wonder at the way her autistic son looks at life through a lens shared by nobody else in the family.

—BEDFORD JOURNAL

Someone I'm With Has Autism

CARRIE CARIELLO

Cover design: Lyn Silarski and Sid Hall
Book design: HobblebushDesign (www.hobblebush.com)

Publisher's Cataloging-in-Publication

Cariello, Carrie.
Someone I'm with has autism / by Carrie Cariello.
pages cm
ISBN 978-0-9847927-5-7
ISBN 978-0-9847927-7-1

1. Cariello, Carrie—Family. 2. Autistic children—United States—Biography. 3. Parents of autistic children—United States—Biography. 4. Families—United States. 5. Autistic children—Family relationships. I. Title.

RJ506.A9C3744 2015 618.92'8588200922
QBI14-600193

Portions of this book have previously appeared in various online publications. Some of the names in this collection have been changed.

Riddle Brook Publishing LLC, Bedford NH
www.riddlebrookpublishing.com
www.carriecariello.com

For my mother,
who always said never to write anything down
you wouldn't want
the whole world to read.

Contents

Part Two: Community

Part Three: Bajillions

Foreword: It's Not About the Autism

I have an eight-year-old son with autism, and when he turned four, I left my position in investment banking to become a stay-at-home father.

I had accepted a new position, one I would come to both love and hate, and autism was the lens through which I would soon view nearly everything about it. I was now, whether I realized it or not, "raising autism."

That would become the label I would cope with for the next several years. I found myself, whether I liked it or not, the tour guide on the journey that was "raising autism." It's had its ups. It's had its downs. It's had its laughs and tears. Yet the journey continues.

There is a famous saying in the autism community: "If you've met one kid with autism, you've met one kid with autism." It is an oft-repeated mantra meant to celebrate the uniqueness and individuality of this broad spectrum. It is also a very frustrating, dismissive answer when you are asking questions. I didn't want to raise autism anymore, I wanted to raise my son. Yet a frustrating shrug of the shoulders doesn't help when you are asking a question, when you are looking for help. I needed a guide. Someone to teach me. Someone to educate me. Someone to hold my hand. Someone to stand between myself and harm's way.

So I started reading blogs.

Love always protects us in all the dark places we must travel, and I knew it would be no different in this case. What I wasn't prepared for—but was thrilled to find—was the amazing community I would be exposed to. Parents, bloggers, adult self-advocates, therapists, teachers, friends, and doctors were new rocks for me to polish, glean, and simply rest upon.

I read a lot of blogs by parents of children on the spectrum. I read them to educate myself. I read them to entertain myself. I read them to fill my own empathetic reservoir. One day I was reading a blog written by a mom that was about the absurdity of making a business card, something she could pass out to complete strangers that would explain that her son had autism. I was struck with the simplicity of her business card idea, and yet also by the complexity of what it said: "Someone I'm with has autism: It's complicated." Amen.

That blog was written by Carrie Cariello.

I scrambled to read everything she had ever written. I picked up a copy of her book, *What Color is Monday?* I devoured her blog posts. Carrie was not only a brilliant writer with a strong voice and magical sense of humor, she was a mom I quickly admired. She just got it.

But there was something deeper for me—her boy. I enjoyed the stories of her husband and the other kids and the dog, but I was drawn to Jack. I was mesmerized by Jack. I could not take my metaphorical eyes off him, probably because he was just like my son (coincidentally also named Jack). Carrie, in her telling of her son's personal "hero's journey," was guiding my own.

Carrie wrote a blog posting once about what she wanted for her son: what she wanted from teachers, what she wanted from future employers, what she wanted from his friends, what she wanted from the world for her son with autism. Her answer was immaculate:

"I just want you to know him."

She wasn't asked why she shares her journey with the world, yet she answered it so succinctly with that one simple statement. Carrie shares her journey with the world so that we can get to know her son. And I, for one, am fulfilled by knowing him.

The adventures of Jack and his family are brilliantly weaved throughout these pages. The laughs and the tears are all here. The quirks of confidence and the darkness and fear of a family navigating a terrifying world are here, too. However, Carrie will hold your hand with grace, humor, compassion, and empathy, and stand between you and harm's way in all those dark places you must travel.

I am forever indebted to Carrie for writing. She is a wonderful storyteller. A truly caring mother. A dedicated and loving wife. An appropriately stern matriarch.

Most importantly, Carrie is an educator. She said she has one goal through her writing and asks the world one thing, to get to know her son.

His name is Jack. And he is amazing.

—Jordan Capell

Introduction: Sleep

The bedroom door opens with a creak and a very young boy steps out into the darkened hallway. Just shy of three, this boy is tall for his age and sturdy in build, wearing multi-colored pajamas that are too short for him. He quietly steps to the landing of the staircase and begins to descend.

The house is new to him, and although he remembers the layout from the day before, his ears perk up at the unfamiliar sounds of a humming refrigerator and a creaking floor. He makes his way downstairs, sidestepping moving boxes and hanging garment bags, and his eyes alight on the object he's been coveting since he first saw it a day earlier: the spidery chandelier with hanging crystals shaped like teardrops. He quickly climbs onto one of the chairs surrounding the table and hoists himself underneath the sparkling fixture. Standing at full height, he unscrews each of its half-dozen light bulbs and drops them to the top of the oak table where they roll about and fall to the floor. One shatters.

From table height he spies the peculiar machine he watches his parents use daily, and from which they pour large, tantalizing cups of hot liquid. With no one around to say to him *don't touch*, he noiselessly hops from the table and pads over to the counter. He boldly pushes the button and watches the red light blink on. Then, nothing.

Unable to sustain his attention, the mystifying appliance is left behind; the small boy wanders a little around the first floor and finally meanders over to the double front doors, yet to receive the child locks of his previous home. He easily works the lever-shaped door knob and steps wordlessly into the chilly April morning. He crosses the front lawn in his bare feet, and holding his arms aloft begins spinning to an unnamed song.

The boy in this story is Jack.

At the time Jack had only a dozen or so words in his three-year-old's vocabulary. He couldn't tell us what he was looking for on that cool April morning. He never thought to wake one of us up for help navigating a house that was new to him. And although his communication has flourished since that very first night in New Hampshire, he still can't put words to this memory.

How silent he was.

As many parents of kiddos with autism know, sleep is one of the many things this tricky disorder messes with. Issues like interrupted circadian rhythms, irregular melatonin production, and anxiety all contribute to irregular sleep patterns and nighttime antics. Autism can make a child wake up and go to sleep and wake up and call out and wake up and put *Baby Einstein* movies in the DVD player and wake up and crack eggs into a bowl and then doze off on the floor and wake up again to start the whole thing over. And once you smarten up and put locks and gates and alarms on every door and window in your house, he will just stand in his crib and bang his hands against the wall and repeat words like *pancake* over and over and over.

At some point, Jack's nocturnal wandering stopped, and it was replaced with early morning jumping and hopping, a hallmark of his anxiety. Around 4:00 a.m. he'd start rocking and chanting in his bed as panic about *toilets* and *fire drills* and *the wind chill factor* raced through his six-year-old body, his wooden headboard thumping against the wall.

And now?

Well, these days—with the help of melatonin—his early-morning anxiety is resolved, his sleep patterns more regular. Jack no longer wakes a hundred times a night or gets up to roam wordlessly through the house.

But he is an incredibly early riser and (to the dismay of six other people who live in our house) he is also an incredibly *loud* early riser. We hear him slamming his dresser drawers as he rifles through them for his socks and pants and shirt. Then he bumbles down the hallway, muttering incoherently to himself about *chorus* and *waffles* and *the capital of Idaho*, bangs the door to our room open, and stands at the side of my bed, fully dressed, glasses perched high on his nose, until I open my eyes.

This happens every morning between 5:58 and 6:11. Precisely. Every morning.

When this first began I was annoyed. I tried to convince him to go back to sleep or snuggle with me or go to Joe's side of the bed—anything to get just five more minutes out of the night.

"No," he'd command. "We are time to get up now."

So I do. And he trails close behind me as I make my way into the bathroom. He perches on the edge of the tub and watches as I wash my face, pull my hair back. And all the while he talks.

In his robotic voice he asks about my makeup and reports that his new library book is boring and tells me how small Nicaragua is. His thoughts are disconnected and disjointed, and in the quiet darkness of morning, with only the faint sound of Joe snoring or the refrigerator humming downstairs, I can hear just how unusual his syntax is.

"Jack, why don't you go make your bed while you wait for me?"

"Because no. I am hard at making my bed."

But in those fifteen minutes or so before the rest of the family wakes up, Jack doesn't have to struggle to keep up as words and sentences and laughter flow around him like warm, sticky honey out of a hive. He doesn't have to wade through the bee-like buzz of confusing conversation, sorting through phrases and comments to decipher sarcasm and jokes and irony.

Every once in a while, if I stay quiet enough and don't move too quickly, he will move past *why is that lipstick called desert sand* and *I do not like* Magic Tree House to reveal the private inner sanctum of his racing mind. He will say things like *this autism is stuck in me* and *I don't know how to being around people.*

He will reveal himself.

A few months ago he sat with his long legs crossed and told me, "When I was born-ded, I didn't know who you were. But then I looked. At you. And I said, that is her. That is my mother." Hearing him put words to a memory, I felt like the luckiest person awake in the world. I felt like the unusual sleep patterns of autism didn't matter quite as much anymore. They give me this way of being with him.

Yesterday morning I opened my eyes at dawn to see him standing over me, straight and tall like a soldier. Only this time, instead of his usual khakis and striped shirt, he was wearing his plush blue bathrobe.

"Jack," I whispered in the gray light. "Why are you wearing your robe?"

"Because! I can't wait," he shouted at the top of his lungs. "I can't want to wake anyone up by SLAMMING MY DRAWERS!"

He's definitely not stealthy anymore, I thought to myself as I swung my legs over the side of the bed and rooted around my closet for my own black robe.

But he's also no longer silent.

Part One: Family

As many of you know, my first book, *What Color Is Monday? How Autism Changed One Family for the Better*, was a memoir about our life with five kids and autism.

This book is a little different. Although still about our life with the kids and autism and all of that good stuff, it's a collection of essays from my blog, www.carriecariello.com, as well as some new pieces.

When I reviewed all of the posts and essays I'd written over the past two years, I was struck by how much our family has changed since the first memoir. Oh, sure, Rose continues to talk in a raspy voice and Henry is still the loudest person I've ever met, but Charlie has started reading chapter books, and now Joey needs to buy his sneakers in the men's section. Jack is in the fifth grade.

One big development stands out above the others: the kids know about Jack's autism. And Jack knows about Jack's autism. In some ways this has redefined the dynamics of our family. It's as though we had a warm pot of stew bubbling on the stove and we took the lid off to examine all of the yummy ingredients inside: bright orange carrots and rich brown gravy, rigidity and stimming and executive functioning. And then all of us decided that we love stew. We love autism.

But Jack? Well, as you'll read, he's not as impressed with autism as the rest of us are.

My essays are written in real-time, so to speak, and one of my flaws as a writer—of which I have many—is failing to write for the uninformed reader. Basically, I assume you already know everything about us: how Charlie dreams of dragons and Henry still has a little lisp and Jack loves pancakes. But if you're new to this story and our family then you probably don't, so allow me to introduce you to the cast of characters.

I am married to a man named Joe. He is a dentist. I write a lot about our marriage, but none of those pieces made it into this book, so I'll just tell you that Joe is kind and strong and good. He is Italian and has very dark, wavy hair and brown eyes. Sometimes we disagree about autism and parenting and the best way to drive to New Jersey, but at the end of the day he makes me laugh the hardest.

Joe and I have four boys and one girl. Oldest to youngest they are: Joey, age eleven; Jack, age ten; Charlie, age eight; Rose, age seven; and Henry, age five.

Things it may help to know about Jack: Joe and I call him Jack-a-boo. He struggles with tremendous anxiety and for the longest time he was terrified of dogs. Now he's less terrified, but I'm getting ahead of myself.

Rose calls him Jackie.

Jack loves Bertucci's. It's been his go-to restaurant since he was about five. If you ask him where he wants to go for breakfast, lunch, dinner, afternoon tea, or dessert, he will shout, "Bertucci's!" This is equal parts annoying and endearing to me.

We call our minivan the Red Hot Chili Pepper.

I use the expression *light my eyelashes on fire* a lot. This is equal parts annoying and endearing to my editor. I want you to know I argued for each and every instance where it shows up in this book because some things are just worth fighting for.

This section of the book is all about family. I like to think of the kids as little mirrors for Jack. The four of them are the smallest reflection of the person he'd like to be: empathetic and social and funny and athletic. Because of them, he sees and he watches and he tries. Time and time again they pull him away from autism's compelling inner universe and into their larger world of *kickball* and *family dance parties* and *restaurants other than Bertucci's*.

Joey, Charlie, and Rose each know Jack has autism. How much they understand of this diagnosis varies: Joey grasps the full concept of spectrum disorder, while Charlie relates it to Jack needing an aide to help him navigate elementary school. And Rose calls it his "owt-ism," which is about the cutest thing ever: "Jackie has the owt-ism and it makes him jump around a lot."

Although five-year-old Henry does not have a name for his older brother's jumping or unusual speech pattern, he seems to sense a difference. I don't think it will be long before he figures it all out for himself.

Jack himself is just learning about his own diagnosis, a discovery that has been both painful and astonishing to him. As he continues to process the idea that he is different in many ways, his three brothers and one sister are his safety net. Through a combination of love, acceptance, and good old-fashioned sibling exasperation, they normalize his autism. And by that, I mean they make him feel normal.

By sharing our story, I hope that each of you touched by autism will feel a bit more normal, too. Because here, in our house, he isn't a boy with an *individualized education plan* or a *para* or a *diagnosis*. He's simply a brother who insists on pancakes every Saturday morning. He is Jack.

Or Jackie, for one pink little girl.

It Doesn't Mean About the Mug

"Oh no!" Jack shrieked from where he was standing at the kitchen sink. I rushed over and saw one of Joe's dark blue mugs, now missing its curved handle, broken when Jack had tried to rinse the hot chocolate out of it.

"I broke it I broke it I BROKE IT! I broke Daddy's mug," he yelled, holding his hands on his ears.

"Jack," I said. "It is no big deal, really. Just relax."

"Can we glue it?" he asked, holding the handle-less mug up.

But I told him, no, it was broken for good, we would toss it in a plastic bag and throw it away.

"No! No. No. Daddy will be upset."

I didn't know what all of the fuss was about. We have something like nine hundred and ten of these cobalt blue mugs, each emblazoned with the name of Joe's dental practice, and frankly I'd like to break a few more so I'd have an excuse to buy the white ones I've been eyeing at Pottery Barn. They match my dishes better.

I promised that his father would absolutely *not* be upset,

then tried to soothe him by pointing to the rest of our mugs in the cabinet—and on the counter (and in the garage).

"But he LOVES them all!" he whimpered.

I couldn't console him. He cried off and on all afternoon, calming down just long enough to announce, "But tomorrow. Tomorrow I have art." And I agreed that, yes, he *did* have art and, yes, art *is* just so much fun, before heading back into the kitchen to make meatloaf for dinner.

The following afternoon he flew off the bus with a package wrapped in tissue paper.

"The mug!" he cried. "It's here!" Once we were in the kitchen he set it down carefully and unwrapped it with some ceremony.

"With this mug. First it was for you. Now it is for Daddy."

Together we all clustered around and admired the lumpy blue-green mug.

"Nice job, Jack," Joey said.

"It look like a bowl!" Henry offered.

"Jackie, you worked hard on this! Daddy will love it!" Rose chimed in.

Right away Jack decided he needed to test it out for himself before giving it to Joe, and he busied himself with his hot chocolate routine.

Soon he was sitting at the counter reviewing all of the mug's qualities: "You can drink SOUP from it!" or "Hot chocolate tastes GOOD in it!" and, "It is safe in the DISHWASHER!"

Then, swiping at his mouth with his sleeve; "It DRIPS a little." He looked up. "But do not tell him. Dad. I want to be it a surprise," he commanded me with his clipped tone and unusual syntax.

As he gingerly put the mug into the sink, he turned to me with a twinkle in his eye. "Did you. Have you. Seen. A NOTE? On your bed."

Leaning against the counter I vaguely remembered Joe coming to bed late the night before and, as he pulled back the covers, a sheet of paper falling gently to the floor.

"Uh huh," I told Jack. And as soon as he wandered up to the playroom to start the karaoke machine, I headed upstairs and found the piece of paper, a little crumpled from where it had slid under the bed.

It doesn't mean about the mug it said. *I have pottery from art class at school for you.*

Doesn't mean about the mug? I thought. What is he trying to say? But when I asked him to explain, his face snapped shut. "I am not talking. About this anymore."

Joe had a meeting after work that night, so the kids and I had soup and sandwiches for dinner. Jack lingered in the kitchen after the others had gone up to take their showers, watching me load the dishwasher and wipe down the counters. "Where? Where does Dad get his coffee mug in the morning? From the cabinet or the counter?" he asked, referring to the collection of coffee cups we keep clustered around the Keurig.

"Um," I said, trying to remember Joe's morning coffee habits. "Well, I think the cabinet, Jack-a-boo. Why?"

"That is where I will put this one. To surprise him. In the morning." And carefully he rearranged the dozen or so mugs on the shelf—ones that say *Number One Bowler* and *Lehigh Construction* and *Hot 98.7*—to place his front and center. Satisfied, he turned without a word and hopped out of the kitchen.

For no reason at all I felt a lump in my throat. I didn't know why. Kids the world over present their parents with homemade gifts—ornaments and candle holders and picture frames—sometimes for birthdays or holidays, sometimes just because. So why did this misshapen little cup affect me so much? Why did I walk over to the cabinet and open the door and stand staring at it once I was alone in my darkened kitchen?

I think this is why.

At this point one of Jack's biggest issues is *theory of mind*, or the concept that other people have thoughts, ideas, or opinions that are different from his.

Let's say, for example, that Jack really really, *really* loves hot chocolate. He thinks and talks a lot about hot chocolate: which brand is his favorite, the best marshmallows to layer on the top, how you should always add a few ice cubes before you drink it so it will cool off.

And then one afternoon you casually remark that you don't really care for hot chocolate, that you had it once when you were a little girl and it burned your mouth and you've never really liked it since.

Right away young Jack's brain begins to short-circuit in a way that suggests his head may explode. He starts to jump and stim and chant things like *how can you not like hot chocolate I love hot chocolate hot chocolate hot chocolate I can't believe you don't like hot chocolate HOT CHOCOLATE!*

This can go on for hours. And if his own head does not, in fact, explode—if it stays firmly attached to his neck in one round piece—he will do everything in his power to make sure yours explodes instead.

But with this mug Jack's rigid mind opened just a crack. He theory-ed, if you will, enough to realize that Joe might be sad to come home and find one of his mugs broken.

Right alongside Jack's theory of mind is his *cognitive flexibility*, his mental ability to adjust thinking or attention in response to changing goals or environmental stimulus.

This is really just a fancy way of saying he doesn't switch gears very easily.

In everyday terms it means this: If you say *Hey everybody let's go see* Frozen *at Chunky's at 5:45*, and you get to Chunky's Cinema at 5:15 so you are nice and early for the movie but there are still no more seats left, Jack will have a little, hmmm, how shall I say it? a little trouble adjusting to the idea that we have to come back another day.

(Note: *Trouble* can mean anything from screaming, kicking, bouncing into walls, beating his own head, and ordering unsuspecting Chunky's employees to find seven seats *right this minute*.)

But with this mug, he adjusted. Obviously the class had been working on the project for some time because pottery is not formed and baked and glazed in a single day. And when the handle came off his father's blue mug, Jack switched his gears to replace the broken one.

I've often thought that Jack does not appear to experience a full range of emotions in the same way you or I might. Sure, he gets mad if I take away the Wii and sad if there isn't a snow day when he thought there would be and happy when we all go bowling, but his spectrum disorder seems to prohibit his emotional pendulum from swinging widely across a landscape of feelings that often include shame and humility and empathy and amusement.

But with this mug the pendulum swung a little wider. After the initial shock of having broken his dad's mug, he cycled through a new set of emotions: sorrow, regret, and (to some degree) grief. And then excitement, anticipation, glee—my normally transparent son kept a secret and surprised his father.

It almost makes me want to open my own pottery studio.

But maybe I don't have to. Maybe—just maybe—this is a starting point for Jack, a chance for him to understand that other people prefer hot cider to hot chocolate and feel the uncomfortable feeling of regret and keep giggly childhood secrets.

With this mug, I hope.

The Pocket in Our Brain

"When can I get the Wii back. I need it. I need the Wii," Jack begged as he trailed me from room to room. One week earlier I had decided that all five children were going to detox from the Wii. It wasn't pretty. There may have been some yelling involved.

In fact, it wasn't just the Wii gaming system. In what could be called an overzealous/brave/stupid moment of parenting zeal, we also took away the iPad and the television.

Some of us detoxed better than others.

"I need the Wii. Wii now!"

Out of sheer courtesy and consideration, I have provided only the abridged version of this conversation. Because it actually went on for A LOT longer. Hour after blessed hour he followed me around, pleading and whining for the small square console I'd "removed" from the television.

Normally a ninety-second conversation with Jack goes something like this:

Did you know Uncle Frank was born before Hawaii became a state Dusty Springfield's music is considered pop but Mary J. Blige is called soul why does Santa eat cookies are we ever going to visit California tomorrow it will be hot in Guam.

Inside Jack's soft, brown, closely cropped head, I picture a teeny-tiny train running along a miniature track. Most of the time this train runs smoothly—albeit quickly—through stations that might cover music or spiders, dates or license plates.

But every now and again the Jack-train stalls. It gets delayed, or idles. Instead of rushing past Dusty Springfield and over to Guam, it sputters to a halt at pancakes or eyeglasses or the schedule of Scooby-Doo episodes on TV.

Or the Wii.

My son can't handle a *maybe* or *we'll see* or *I'm not sure yet, Jack.* He craves certainty and the opposite—ambiguity—makes him nuts. If there is no definitive response to his looping questions or repeated demands, if we don't know what time we'll have dinner or when the Mobil Mart opens for the day or if we'll see the new movie *Turbo* on Friday or Saturday, the train just revs in place, wheels spinning and engine grumbling.

"Jack," I said softly, bracing myself for the storm. "I do not think we are getting the Wii back. I think we are done with it."

You can imagine the tantrum that came next. I won't go into specific details.

Okay. Maybe I will.

"WHAAAAT!! No Wii back! But I need it. I need the Wii," he cried, flapping his hands in the air.

I tried every tactic. I asked him if he wanted to go for a

bike ride. I proposed painting. I offered to play one of our favorite games, Boggle. Nothing worked to slow his descent into what we call "the red zone," a point of severe distress. Just as he dropped to the floor kicking and screaming, I suggested a cooking project to take his mind off video games, to nudge the train along its proverbial track.

"Hey, Jack. How about we bake some cookies?"

"Can we have the Wii after we bake?"

Sigh.

Exasperated, frustrated, and quickly approaching a tantrum myself, I blurted, "You know what? You need to put your thoughts about the Wii away. Put them . . . in the pocket. The pocket in your brain!"

As soon as I said it my stomach lurched a little. Pocket in the brain? What a disgusting idea. I instantly pictured the looping grey grossness of the cerebral cortex with a denim pocket stitched in it, but it got his attention. He looked up at me bewildered and repeated, "A pocket? In my brain?"

It was just the foothold I needed. I explained that, yes, everyone's brain has a pocket in it, a place where we store ideas and thoughts that we don't want to forget about, but we don't need to keep thinking about over and over.

I tapped the side of my own head, right above my right ear, to show him where I keep my pocket.

"What is in there. In your pocket," he asked in his monotone, hopping from one foot to the other.

What is in there? I paused for a second and considered all the little things I think about over and over: if I should grill the pork chops or bake them for dinner, if I should sign Rose up for gymnastics again, if I did the right thing by taking the Wii away, whether or not I should buy new towels from Lands' End. When I really thought about it, I could absolutely relate to Jack's mind getting stuck because I have my own train to deal with.

"Well, sometimes I can't stop thinking about little stuff, like what to make for dinner or what time I should go to Crossfit. If we should get new sneakers now or wait until school starts. If we should take Grandma out for her birthday or—"

"All right," he interrupted. "Stop talking about it. Let's bake those cookies."

And so we busied ourselves with pan, bowl and recipe. As I helped him measure and pour and stir, Joey and Charlie got out the Boggle, and before long all three boys were playing, the Wii forgotten for the time being.

Throughout the week I used the pocket-in-the-brain idea to jog Jack whenever his train got stuck. When he started to beg for the iPad or ask the third question about brown recluse spiders or if it was going to rain out, I would tap my head and tell him to tuck it away, to put that thought in his pocket for now. And it seemed to work; each time he'd pause for a second before moving on to something else. It was like watching that little train start up and gain speed, trundling past the roadblocks and obstructions that sometimes stalled it.

But maybe the ultimate pocket success was with seven-year-old Charlie. No stranger to worrying and preoccupation himself, dark-haired Charlie could not stop talking about swimming in the town pool. Every day he'd ask when we were going, if we could stay long, how many trips he could take down the blue spiral slide.

We were in the car, headed to the grocery store, when my dark-haired boy announced, "I think I'm going to put the town pool in the pocket in my brain. I am tired of thinking about it and I need my brain to stop."

I looked at him in the rearview mirror and noticed how his body—tense and nervous about the *why can't we go to the town pool today* argument a moment before—relaxed.

And it occurred to me that the pocket in our brain can provide a break, restfulness, peace from the barrage of thoughts and ideas and opinions we bombard ourselves with all day, from pork chops for dinner to the town pool to beige or eggshell towels. It's a release. And then there is space, room for our minds to dream, to imagine, to think in color.

I was still reveling in my pocket problem-solving victory that night at dinner when I decided to take the concept just a smidge further. I suggested that maybe the pockets in our brains have zippers attached to them, to keep our thoughts safely tucked inside. Jack, however, was not on board.

"Stop talking about that dumb POCKET! It is ANNOYING ME!"

From across the table, Joey smirked at me and suggested, "Mom, maybe it's time to put the pocket in your brain in the pocket in your brain."

They all screamed laughing. Henry slapped a chubby hand on the table and chortled around a mouthful of corn, "Put da pocket IN DA POCKET!" Rose giggled so hard she squirted milk out of her mouth.

These kids are so not getting that Wii back.

Shoe Shopping

On our way to pick out new sneakers for my three oldest boys, and in between answering questions about license plates, car models, and how long it would take to drive to Florida, I may have flippantly said something to Jack like *yeah sure maybe we'll go to Bertucci's for lunch we'll see.*

But first we needed to get sneakers. On we went, to the overcrowded shoe store teeming with parents and kids.

Jack hates this store. It's very loud and confusing, and every single time he picks out a pair of sneakers he wants, it seems they don't have his size, so we have to start the whole process over again. This year, on top of all that, and about halfway through negotiating neon-orange versus scarlet-red Nikes, we heard a dog barking. From *inside* the store. Apparently the owners had gotten a new labradoodle (or whatever those breeds are called), and they keep him by the cash register.

Jack hates dogs.

Eventually each of the boys decided on the perfect pair of sneakers and we left. On the two-block walk back to the car we passed a restaurant with outdoor seating. "Hmmmm . . ."

I thought to myself. "That would be a nice spot to eat." All at once I badly wanted to sit outside with my boys and enjoy the beautiful summer sunshine. I wanted to drink an iced tea and listen to them chatter about whatever it is they felt like chattering about, and to hear Jack point out different license plates as cars drove by. I did not want to go to Bertucci's.

But Jack did.

As soon as I suggested stopping at the sidewalk tables for lunch, he went haywire. Already ramped up from a visit to a shoe store that didn't have his sneaker size (but did have a dog), it didn't take long for him to reach the red zone. He started jumping around and waving his arms, begging for "Bertucci's! You said Bertucci's!" I explained that I said *maybe* Bertucci's, but sometimes we need to be flexible; plans change, and doesn't this look fun?

(At that moment, it was looking like anything *but* fun.)

While Jack fumed and stomped around the sidewalk, the other two boys quietly seated themselves at the black wrought iron table. Charlie, with wide dark eyes, watched Jack's tantrum as Joey fiddled with his napkin and looked through the cocktail menu, probably wishing he was old enough for a mojito. They're used to these scenes, but they never really get used to these scenes. And neither do I.

When the server stopped by to take our drink order, Jack clapped his hands over his ears and hissed, "Stop it. Now." And then he started to rock in his seat and whine at a very high pitch. She looked unnerved.

I wanted to scream at him. I wanted to squeeze his arm and shake him until he stopped his hideous keening and settled down. I wanted him to stop it. Now.

I was very tempted to pay for my iced tea and milks and flee, to run to the Red Hot Chili Pepper, buckle them in, and trundle over to the nearest Bertucci's for a relaxing meal with my autistic son and his two wary brothers. The words *let's just go* were on the tip of my tongue. It wouldn't have been the first time we'd left somewhere because Jack was distraught.

But then Joey said something to snap the picture into focus for me:

"Mom. I think the school program shows Jack how to only have a disappointment-free life. You know, because he always gets to be first in line and stuff. It's like he doesn't know that life is disappointing sometimes."

His comment couldn't have been timelier. In that instant, I realized what I needed to do.

I needed to make an effort to flex Jack's rigid mind, to help him grow and change even if it meant being uncomfortable myself. Lemony iced tea and a sidewalk lunch aside, I needed to help him tolerate disappointment because, to quote a nine-year-old, life really *is* disappointing sometimes. I am Jack's mother and this is my job.

And so we stayed.

It wasn't pretty; Jack continued to rant and rail against the injustice of outdoor seating and pleading his case for Bertucci's. At one point he banged on the table hard enough to bounce the silverware. But I stood my ground, alternating between soothing him and pointing out the different cars driving by, the rarely-glimpsed Texas license plate in the middle of New Hampshire and the spoiler on the back of the Nissan Sentra. And slowly, through the course of the meal, he relaxed.

And then, a milestone.

For the first time, Jack verbally acknowledged a change in his mood and body; after a few bites of chicken fingers and a long cool drink of his milk, he said, "I feel good now." He started to shout out license plates at lightning speed; "Mom! Florida. I see Florida. On that Dodge Dakota." I slumped in my chair, relieved the outburst was over and marveling at this small victory.

On the drive home, in between sound bites of "Georgia!" and "Massachusetts again?" I asked him if he'd had fun in the restaurant after all. Yes, he agreed. It was okay.

"But tomorrow I want to go to Bertucci's."

Baby steps.

Can I Ask You Something?

We took the kids to Outback Steakhouse for dinner last week, and after two trips to the bathroom, Jack said he needed to go again. "No," Joe told him. "You can't possibly need to go again."

"But. I have to!"

"Sit down and wait," Joe suggested. "Your dinner will be here in just a minute."

"But. But!" Jack shouted. "It's important to listen to your BODY!"

"Yes," Joe agreed. "And what is your body telling you?"

I was bent over my salad, picking out the onions, when I heard that question. My head snapped up and we locked eyes. We both braced ourselves for Jack's answer.

Now, I know there is no such thing as a dumb question. I was raised on the motto *the one who asks the most, knows the most*, and I believe that to be true. But there are some things you just don't ask Jack.

Anything to do with bodily functions, appearances, age, death, gravestones, and howler monkeys. And while we're at it, I would also stay off the subject of whether Andrea

Bocelli is better than The Four Seasons. Oh, and the speed limit on the New York State Thruway.

A couple of years ago we had a barbecue at our house with Joe's family. His niece walked in just as we were about to sit down for dinner, dressed in a short black skirt and tight tank top. As we gathered around the table, she noticed Jack staring at her and smiled at him coquettishly, all teenage curves and fashion.

"Jack, how do I look?"

I flew across the table, using both hands to snatch up things to put in his mouth—carrot stick, potato chip, margarita—anything to keep him from answering.

"You look," he considered, "squeezed."

My sister-in-law still giggles that she's never seen me move so fast.

With five kids, my life somewhat revolves around questions. I am no stranger to them. All day long they pepper me with questions, questions, questions. Who, what, when, where, why?

Then there's the double question, the "Mom can I ask you a question?" question, *before* the actual question.

If I'm in a good mood I usually answer with a cheery, "Sure, ask me anything!" If it's been a long afternoon, I might clench my teeth and say something like, "You DON'T NEED to ask me if you can ask me something. JUST ASK."

And if it's been a really long afternoon and it's the end of summer, I just might say something like, "If you ask me one more thing, I'm going to LIGHT MY EYELASHES ON FIRE." (I'm totally kidding! I would never say something like that to my kids!)

(I may have said something like that to my kids.)

But oh, the questions.

Within a forty-five-minute time frame, I can answer as many questions as this:

"Am I allergic to lemons?"

"Did Elvis Presley have kids?"

"Can we go to Friendly's for lunch?"

"Where are my shoes?"

"I have more stwa-bewwies?"

"Am I taller than Jack?"

"Can we buy roller skates?"

"What are woller skates?"

"What is the weather in Guam today?"

"Why not?"

"Can I get the Volcano at Friendly's?"

"Whaddya mean I'm just allergic to good behavior?"

"Did you use your Macy's charge last week?"

(Okay, that last question was from Joe. But still: SO MANY QUESTIONS!)

And Jack. When he's not pronouncing (*Life cereal has more grams of sugar than Honeycomb)* or announcing (*Dusty Springfield recorded "Son of a Preacher Man" when Aunt Elaine was eight years old*) or denouncing (*The movie screens in Cinemagic are too big*), he's asking questions.

All the livelong day, questions.

They range from the practical (*What time are we eating dinner?*) to the existential (*Why are you thirty-eight?*). From the religious (*What does heaven look like?*) to basic fact-finding (*How many people live in Texas?*). If he doesn't hear the answer he likes, he'll repeat the question over and over and over again. Just the other day he asked me what time Mobil Mart opens in the morning. The conversation went like this:

> *Jack: "What time does the Mobil Mart on Elm Street in Manchester open?"*
>
> *Me: "I don't know Jack."*
>
> *Jack: "But what time does it open."*
>
> *Me: "See, the thing is, I don't know."*
>
> *Jack: "Do you think it opens at six?"*
>
> *Me: "I. Don't. Know."*
>
> *Jack: "How about seven."*
>
> *Me: "I HAVE NO IDEA!"*
>
> *Jack (indignant): "Stop talking loud. It hurts my ears."*

Twenty-seven minutes later:

> *Jack: "Mom. Mom. What time does the Mobil Mart open. In Manchester."*

Once I tried to keep track of how many questions he asked in a single day. I stopped counting at eighty-three, which doesn't sound like much except he was out of the house at karate camp for the entire afternoon.

But lately I'm starting to read the queries a little differently, to understand that sometimes children reveal a lot about themselves with their requests.

Mom, can I skip dinner? is a good sign Charlie has the stomach bug.

Mom, can I always live here? With you and Daddy? tells me Rose is hoping to keep her happy childhood in place, intact. That she wants to stay a little girl for as long as she can.

On our way out of Hannaford's the other day, four-year-old Henry asked me poignantly, "I was good there? At the store?" and I realized how much I'd been harping on him lately to behave, to be quiet, to be good. After his question I resolved to praise him more.

Underneath all of Jack's questions I can see his anxiety winding around his soul and psyche like a cool, dry snake. Eyes downcast, he begs to know when he's going to die, when we're going to die, if our car is going too fast, when the wind chill will drop. And if I take a moment to listen, what I really hear is *I am scared I am nervous I am anxious.*

Questions are Jack's dialogue, his discourse, his way of figuring out our world of life and death and music and spiders, his way of orienting himself.

Over the weekend we were packing for a trip to the lake with some friends, and I suggested Jack bring along my mini-speakers so he could listen to his music on the hour-long drive.

"But. But," he stammered, searching for words. "Won't that. Irritate the others. To listen to my music?"

With this one monotone question, I realized he's continuing to march along a progressive path, a trajectory that may someday catapult him a little beyond the boundaries of Autism Spectrum Disorder: he's starting to care about what other people think and feel.

Slowly, he's realizing that yes—YES, JACK!—an hour of Nicki Minaj would certainly irritate the others.

But back to our dinner at Outback.

Maybe you're wondering about how Jack answered Joe's question. And so I'll tell you.

Nine-year-old Jack stood next to our table with his hands on his hips, wearing bright red shorts, a black t-shirt with *I Love Bowling* printed across the front, and an indignant expression. He opened his mouth and shrieked for every blooming onion-eating patron of Outback to hear:

"My body is telling me to GET RID OF THIS DIARRHEA."

Maybe there is such a thing as a dumb question.

How Many Minutes?

Every Memorial Day weekend our family drives to New Jersey to visit Joe's brother Frank at his place near the Jersey shore, and to go to the Cariello's Big Italian Family Reunion. We leave from New Hampshire Saturday morning, drive three hours, stop at the same McDonald's in Connecticut for lunch, then drive another two hours to Frank's house. We hang out there for a little while, then head over to the Point Pleasant boardwalk, where we ride the rides and eat the food and play the games until about midnight.

All of my kids love this tradition, especially Jack.

Jack is one of those beautifully rare birds perched on the spectrum wire who actually likes to travel. He just loves exploring new places and taking pictures and visiting family. Every time we go somewhere he packs up his three different flavors of ChapStick and his nasal spray and his favorite stuffed bunny, and he hops in the car, giddy with excitement. Unfortunately for his travel-mates, he also packs his rigidity, his bossiness, and his anxiety.

On car trips this trifecta of autism symptoms manifests with an ongoing stream of questions that begin with three words: *How many minutes.*

How many minutes until we're in Connecticut?

How many minutes before lunch?

How many minutes until we need to get gas?

How many minutes until I light my eyelashes on fire?

(That last one was mine, in case you weren't sure.)

Apparently, "How many minutes?" is autism's version of "Are we there yet?" and Jack does not care for approximations. He is not interested in the answer, "Oh, I don't know; a little while!" He wants an exact number, and if you don't know it, well, he'll just keep right on asking until you figure it out. Or until you lie.

Joe, I should mention, has the most annoying habit of whispering when the kids ask him something in the car. No, no, that's not right. He doesn't even whisper. It's more that he mouths the words like a mime, sound barely escaping. He can't, it seems, amplify his voice around the wad of gum he keeps in his mouth while he drives.

> *Jack: "How many more minutes. Until we're out of New Hampshire."*
>
> *Joe (in his weird fake mime voice): "About a half hour."*
>
> *Everyone else in the car except me: "An hour and a half how many minutes what I can't hear you what did he say I think I have to go to the bathroom how many more minutes is it can you hear him I can't hear him!"*

Then there's eight-year-old Charlie, who gets carsick

on long drives. Every single time. Right around an hour into the trip he starts to whimper, leans over, and throws up in his lap.

It defies logic, really.

My inability to prepare for this very predictable travel event also defies logic. This year, as I was organizing the matching orange shirts I bought for the boys (so we could keep track of them on the dark boardwalk later that night), Joe suggested that maybe I should bring a change of clothes for Charlie in case he got sick.

"Nah," I waved my hand at him. "That can't happen every time, can it?"

Well, it can and it did. Exactly one hour after we left our house, pretty much right on schedule, he was leaning over and whimpering. The cacophony of voices in the second and third row of the van hit a fever pitch and sounded like this:

> *He's throwing up again I don't feel so well how many minutes until lunch I'm all right it's not too bad oh that is so gross why does he always have to do this?*

In Connecticut we made our usual stop for lunch at that same McDonald's. After a feast of French fries and nuggets, we all posed with a random panda bear who was strolling around passing out sunglasses. Oh, how fun! Yes, fun. After all, this was only three hours into the drive, and despite the carsickness incident, there was still a sparkle to the day, some shine to the trip.

The shine started to wear off about an hour later, when Joe decided we should take a detour through Brooklyn to show the kids the block where his parents met when they were young.

Remember Jack? The guy with autism? Yeah, not a big fan of detours. Detours *bad*. Changes in plans *bad*. Detours and changes in plans lead to a lot more questions about minutes.

> *Jack (shrieking): "How many MINUTES MORE will this take?"*
>
> *Joe (weird fake mime voice): "I don't know, Jack. Maybe twenty."*
>
> *Everyone else in the car except me: "MAYBE? You mean you DON'T KNOW I thought Grandma and Grandpa were always old you are ruining my life does Brooklyn have a brook in it how many more minutes why is it so hard to hear him I think I need to go to the bathroom."*

And this was only Saturday.

By Memorial Day, after four hours at the boardwalk Saturday night and the family reunion all day Sunday and pizza for dinner on the bed at the Hilton Garden Inn and a hotel pool that was closed for maintenance, the sparkle was all but gone.

We loaded up the suitcases and trundled our tired selves into the van. I'm pretty sure I overheard Henry mutter, "This goddamn thing," when he couldn't fasten his seatbelt around himself and the enormous stuffed pig his cousin Jenny had won for him on the boardwalk. But I didn't care. I didn't even flinch. By that point I had stopped parenting altogether.

As I've mentioned, Charlie never gets sick on the ride

home. He does, however, always, always, *always* have to go to the bathroom about an hour after we leave the hotel. This annoys me so much that we have, in fact, learned to prepare for it.

"We can't stop now, Henry just fell asleep! Use the empty Gatorade bottle!"

"Okay, but I have to unbuckle my seatbelt for a second!"

"Fine, make it quick."

Now, Jack takes safety very, very seriously. He does not tolerate nonsense in this area at all. His eagle eyes are always peeled and on the lookout for driving violations which include, but are not limited to: forgotten blinkers, passing on the right, unnecessary honking, texting, dogs without leashes, and of course, unbuckled seatbelts.

While the rest of the kids dozed comfortably, Jack started a full-blown campaign against Charlie's using the Gatorade bottle. It went something like this:

"Dad SLOW DOWN he is unbuckled Charlie hurry up why do you always have to do this how many more minutes will it take you go slower Dad this is so unsafe!"

Then he took a deep breath, was silent for a second, and shrieked:

"Charlie, you are going to DIE NAKED!"

For the rest of the ride home I pretended to be asleep while Joe kept his hands clenched to the wheel and looked straight ahead. He didn't even do his fake mime voice. In fact, he just didn't answer the questions about *how many minutes* at all.

We dragged ourselves across state lines and drove up our

driveway at last. The kids scattered to different corners of the house and Joe went upstairs to lie face down on the bed.

And I was starting to unwind in my office, to chuckle even, about the absurdities of autism and minutes and Gatorade bottles and panda bears. Then Jack burst in and demanded, "How many minutes until dinner?"

Hearts and Words

One afternoon after school Jack sidled up to me as I was working on my computer. "Mrs. Brennan broke my heart today," he said sadly. "I need to move on from her." I turned to pull him onto my lap and ask why, why he was so sad. "Because. She made me finish my work." I explained that every teacher would make him finish his work, and even if his heart felt broken his brain was getting stronger. Without another word he got off my lap and walked out of the room. Turning back to my computer, I congratulated myself for the way I'd handled his complaint. He has to learn that work is a part of school.

On a whim, I emailed his teacher to share the story. Not long after she wrote back, explaining there was more to this, that there had been a misunderstanding that afternoon. His entire class had been heading into another third-grade room for an activity called Word Recognition, and Jack was very excited for two reasons: the girl he has a crush on is in this class, and he adores the other teacher. But, as luck would have it, he was scheduled for speech at exactly the same time and couldn't go.

We all have our own agendas with Jack. His speech therapist wants to teach him how to make conversation, the occupational therapist needs him to grip his pencil the right way and learn how to get his "zoomies" out. His teacher works to help him maintain academic standards and to know how to spell words like *dither* and *segregation*. And Joe and I want him to engage with our family and lead a full life. (And someday, maybe, walk within two feet of a dog without screaming.)

But at the center of this Bermuda triangle of parents and teachers and therapists stands an earnest little boy, a little boy named Jack who desperately wants to hold his pencil right and learn what *dither* means and know how to say *hello how are you* instead of *how many people can your car fit*. He wants to do Word Recognition with the rest of the third graders.

And his heart is fragile.

A few days later we were alone in the car, and Jack asked me if his five-year-old sister, Rose, goes to speech. I said, no, she does not have speech. Next he asked if she has an aide, and I answered that, no, she doesn't have an aide. And then, very quietly, he asked a third question: "Why do I have an aide and other kids don't?" I took a deep breath and stayed silent for a moment. Lacking a clear answer myself, I turned the question on him: "Why do *you* think you have an aide?"

"Because. Some things are hard for me."

I agreed, yes, some things are harder for him. And driving to the grocery store, I was ready to have a full conversation about the things he finds hard, the things he enjoys, the things that scare him. I was ready to talk about his autism.

But, like most conversations with Jack, this one was very brief and ended when he decided it was over. "No more TALKING! Turn up the radio."

Joe and I haven't really considered a strategy for explaining to Jack that he has autism; we figured it will be apparent when he's ready to know. But I have a feeling that the time is coming soon, because slowly but surely Jack is learning that he's not quite like all the others. He's learning he needs an aide to help him navigate his day, and that other kids are mastering the art of pencil-gripping and conversation-making faster than him. He's learning he has to go to speech while everyone else gets to enjoy Word Recognition. And this is breaking his heart.

And though I'm very ready for Jack to learn about his diagnosis, to understand he has a beautiful, mysterious thing called autism, I'm not quite ready for him to know he's different, unusual, not typical.

Because I'm pretty sure those are words he'll recognize.

A Show of Talent

Ten-year-old Joey sauntered into the kitchen where I sat working Jack and Charlie through homework, and announced he was going to audition for the school talent show. "Great!" I said distractedly, with a pencil clenched between my teeth. "What will you do?"

"Oh, you know. I thought I'd lip sync to *Thrift Shop*," he said, referring to the latest charming pop hit by Macklemore, a song about buying clothes in thrift shops and "poppin' some tags" (which apparently means switching the prices to get the already discounted stuff even cheaper). "Henry could even come on stage with me," Joey said. "He could do the part where the little kid says 'Pop some tags!' at the end."

Four-year-old Henry was kneeling on a stool at the counter coloring in his *Batman* book. Excited about the idea of five minutes of fame on the elementary school stage, he raised his fists in the air and started to shout, "I'm gonna pop some TAGS! Yeah!"

I took the pencil out of my mouth and looked up from the worksheet I was explaining to Charlie. "*Thrift Shop*? Get serious. No way are you singing that song. Think of something else." Joey slunk away, annoyed, just as Henry changed his tune to a singsong, "Yeah! GET SERIOUS Jo-Jo!"

After school a few days later, Joey took my hand as we made our way up our long driveway. "I thought of another idea for the talent show," he said. "I want to read my chapter from the book."

When Joey discovered I was writing my first book, *What Color is Monday?*, a book about our family, he asked if he could write a chapter about his relationship with Jack, if he could write about what he calls *autistic brothering*.

He asked to have a voice.

Now he wanted to bring his brotherly voice to life, to read about autistic brothering to his peers and teachers and friends. I agreed it was a great idea, and that night we practiced for the audition the next day.

The following afternoon I picked Joey up from school, and as he rushed out of the gymnasium with the other kids, I asked him how the audition went. "Great!" he said excitedly. "Everyone loved it."

Then, on the drive out of the school parking lot, it hit me. *Jack does not know he has autism.* And now his older brother was about to announce it to the entire school. How was *that* going to work?

Maybe *Thrift Shop* wasn't such a bad idea after all.

Heading home, I watched in the rearview mirror as Jack stimmed in the back seat, squished between his brothers. I saw Joey move his long legs to the side to give Jack some space and tuck his bony elbows in closer so his younger brother could rock from side to side.

Joey was thirteen months old when Jack was born, two weeks shy of walking on his own. And for nine years he's handled his role as the bigger brother with grace, dealing with the tantrums in restaurants, the fits on the school bus, the long nights with a roommate who stims and rocks in the bunk bed beneath him.

Gamely, he wears matching fluorescent yellow shirts to airports and water parks and movies because he has a brother with a tendency to wander.

And buried in Joey's young mind, nestled among the questions about how babies are really made and if Darth Vader is Luke's father and who the Buffalo Bills will pick for their next quarterback, is the shared sentiment that in order for our family to succeed with this tricky spectrum disorder and help Jack reach seemingly unreachable heights, we need to consider autism from every angle. And then we need to open our arms and hearts and lives and let the world examine it, too.

Jack knew all about the talent show. We picked Joey up after rehearsal one afternoon, and on the ride home Jack demanded to know, "What is your TALENT?" Joey answered that he was reading his chapter from the book.

"Reading is NOT A TALENT! Everyone can READ!"

"You mean you HAVE NO TALENT?" Jack went on loudly. "That is TERRIBLE. When I am in fourth grade I will sing," he announced smugly as we all filed into the house.

Well, that should be interesting, I thought to myself as I dropped my keys on the kitchen counter, while Jack continued to worry, "Reading cannot be your TALENT! You have

NO TALENT!" Joey just smiled and shrugged his shoulders as he kicked his sneakers off and bounded up the stairs to the playroom.

Jack knew that Joey was reading from the book. In fact, he knows all about the book and even scanned it a few times, noting there's an entire chapter named after him. But he's never once asked any questions about what it's about, why he's on the cover, why I wrote it.

The night before the show I sat with Joey and reviewed his chapter. Together, we decided to edit a few parts, removing a sentence here and there so that the message of Jack's diagnosis was a little more subtle, nuanced. "Yeah, Mom," Joey said. "I think this is better. This way it's more about what it's like to be his brother, not so much about how he has autism."

Sitting with teachers and kids and parents in the crowded school gym the next morning, I felt anxious, nervous as we waited for the show to start. What if Jack felt embarrassed hearing his name? What if he had a breakthrough and realized he has autism after all, right in the middle of the school talent show?

I scanned the group of fourth graders in the audience and located Joey. Fresh from the barber's the day before, and dressed in the bright blue polo shirt I'd insisted he wear, he looked heartbreakingly young, yet so big at the same time.

At last it was his turn, and just as his older brother took the stage, Jack bounced out of the sea of squirming kids sitting on the floor and into my lap. He clasped his hands around my neck and, pressing his cheek against mine, said, "It is Joey's turn. He will read now."

And so I sat in the muggy gym with my one son's legs draped over mine, nearly reaching the floor, and watched my other son bring our story to life in a folding chair on the stage.

As Jack's bigger brother, I have a lot of responsibilities. One of my natural responsibilities is to try and keep him calm. My parents don't ask me to do this, I do it because I'm his brother. . . .

I glanced through the crowd of kids and saw Rose watching her brother with rapt attention. I found Charlie's dark-haired head, unmoving and still as he listened to Joey describe Jack's fondness for video games, his tendency to tantrum, the way life is hard for his younger sibling. As a family, we listened to Joey describe his own experience with autism.

I try to be the best brother I can. I like him just the way he is. . . .

Once he was finished, he stood up from his seat and took a bow as the audience applauded. Jack turned his mouth to my ear and reported in a mock-whisper, "He is done now. He did a good job," before he bounced back to his seat on the floor.

And so, in the end, we did what we always do: we flexed to autism's demands while keeping our own shape as a family. And Jack was right. Joey did a good job.

After all, maybe reading really isn't that much of a talent. But autistic brothering certainly is.

Sometimes I Am a Fake Mom

One Saturday morning, just as I was placing a K-Cup into the Keurig for my first cup of coffee, eight-year-old Charlie started to tell me about a dream he'd had the night before.

"And then the dragon ate a purple cherry and he started to run so fast. He was running and uh, he was wearing a . . . what do you call that thing again? Where it has no sleeves on your arms? He was wearing a silver shiny . . . Like, shiny! And then . . . uh . . . then . . . let's see . . . "

I know, precious, right? For the first two minutes. After that I felt like I was slowly pulling brightly colored scarves out of a clown's mouth, one silky strand at a time. I began supplying words to speed up the process—"Vest! It's called a vest!"—while trying not to yawn.

Imagine if you were in a meeting at the office and your co-worker started nattering on and on about his dreams. "And then I dreamed I was riding a horse through the woods, and. . . ." Eventually you would say, "Listen, Doug, that's all good and the horse sounds really fun, but we have to get moving along now, so you need to wrap it up."

But you can't do that with kids. They don't get it. They do not possess the skills to *wrap it up*. They are oblivious to the eye roll, the subtle sigh. That's where Fake Mom comes in.

"And then! Then the dragon grew wings. Yellow wings with blue stripes! Well, they were more like zig-zags. Or maybe dots? I can't remember . . . but he was . . . well, he flew in the air so fast. . . ."

Just before I reached for some matches to light my own eyelashes on fire, Fake Mom stepped up and grabbed the reins of the runaway dragon.

"Charlie! What a creative dream! Show me how fast he flew! Can you fly up the stairs and look for a silver vest in the costume box so you can look just like the dragon? Awesome!"

And away the child galloped, flapping his arms and pretending to fly, all the way to the playroom to look for the silver vest. I let out a big sigh, poured half a bottle of vanilla creamer into my coffee, and took a long sip.

(No, we do not own a silver vest. But it kept the young lad busy for almost an hour trying to find it. Fake Mom is shameless.)

With five kids, Fake Mom is essential. She comes in very handy in the grocery store, at the library, while negotiating the radio station in the car.

Me: "Ssshhh . . . let's be quiet! I love this song!"

Ten-year-old: "This song? This is terrible!"

Eight-year-old: "I like Justin Bieber better. Can you find one with Justin Bieber?"

Five-year-old: "Justin BEAVER?"

Nine-year-old: "Justin BIEBER. *He went to jail."*

Six-year-old: "No he didn't! He went to the moon!"

Five-year-old: "The MOON? Justin Beaver go to da MOON? There no wood to chew on DA MOON!"

And just like that, your song is over.

Fake Mom helps me let go of those ridiculous arguments kids love to engage in, like the time Charlie tried to convince me he could walk upside down. "On the ceiling, Mom! Or even in the sky! My legs would do it, I know they would."

My first instinct was to roll my eyes and say something snarky like, "Okay, smartie, why don't you try it while I stand here and watch. And, spoiler alert! we are **NOT** going to the hospital when you fall and crack your head open."

But Fake Mom does not believe in snark. She is snarkless. Instead, she smiles brightly and tells Charlie that maybe he *can* walk upside down. After all, anything is possible! Probably better to wait until he's a little taller to try it, though.

Fake Mom does not fall to the floor in a fit of giggles when Henry shouts, "These goddamn carrots are crunchy!" at the dinner table. Instead, she rearranges her features so they read polite, yet stern. Unaffected. She seizes the teaching moment with a firm, "That is not a nice word. And carrots *are* crunchy, aren't they? Yum!"

Even Rose, who at six years old is easily the most pleasant person I know, sometimes finds herself talking to Fake Mom, especially the time she cornered me to help her pick out an outfit for her upcoming date with her Daddy. (Joe had missed her school's annual father-daughter dance because we were away on vacation, so he promised he'd take her to dinner to make up for it.)

Two days before said date my pink daughter called me into her room under the pretense of helping her find a library book. Then she trapped me. She all but kicked the door closed, then spun around on one foot and began a verbal assault that went something like this:

"Which dress do you think Daddy will like better, the red or the pink? The pink one twirls more but the red one has more flowers. Or maybe the blue dress with a red coat? What's his favorite color? Just look at these silver tights I found! Oh where did I put that lip gloss? I can't even wait to have dinner with Daddy!"

I gaped back at her and slowly lowered myself down on the bed. *Daddy's favorite color?* I felt like saying. *The guy who kept me up all night snoring and dared question the Macy's charge on this month's credit card bill after he went to Vegas? Who cares what his favorite color is?*

At the rate things were unfolding—literally: dresses, tights, and cardigans were unfolding everywhere—Henry was going to get bumped up to favorite child. And that kid is crazy.

Cue Fake Mom . . .

"Rose, I think he would love the blue one. He loves blue! It matches your pretty eyes. Now, stop unfolding all of those tights."

I know you're all waiting for it. You're wondering about Jack. The boy with autism. You're waiting for me to tell you that I'm *never ever never* a fake mom with him. Right? But I'm not going to say anything like that. In fact, I probably use Fake Mom the most with Jack.

Let me give you an example. The elementary school bus comes at 7:09 a.m. and we have three kids who need to wake up, get dressed, pretend to run a toothbrush around their mouths and fingers through their hair, eat breakfast, find the left boot, find the yellow mitten, run down the driveway, and get on board.

About 92% of the time, this goes very smoothly. But the rest of the time? Disaster.

On this particular morning, Jack—normally the most organized—was moving very slowly. "Jack!" I said sharply. "Put your boots on! Where is your backpack? Did you even pack your snack like I asked you? What is taking you so long! Hurry up!"

He covered his ears and shouted, "Shut UP! Stop talking so much!" right back at me. I felt a bubble of anger rise up in my throat.

Fake Mom rescued me. She rescued us. Instead of taking a deep breath and screeching *how dare you talk to me like that you have no respect if I ever talked to my mother that way I'd be dead you are ruining my morning*, I sat down on the bench and took his warm hands in my own.

Fake Mom whispered really quietly in my ear: *take a second, you can miss the bus for once, look at his face, hear his words, stop talking at him.*

"Jack. What do you need?"

"My boot. Is wet. It's wet. Too wet."

And it was. Soaked, in fact, from sledding the day before.

So we settled on sneakers and agreed he'd stay off the icy snow banks for the day. We also agreed that *shut up* is ugly and mean. And after all that, we still made the bus on time.

Sometimes, Fake Mom is the best I can do.

See, Fake Mom reminds me that although I can buy a favorite song on iTunes any old time, I only have so many years left to hear five-year-old Henry lisp the words to Justin Beaver.

Because of Fake Mom, I take a moment to notice the quiet delight in a little girl's eyes when she finally settles on the navy blue dress and glittery silver tights. I see that the boot is too wet, and I can appreciate that every now and again, it's important for a dark-haired boy to believe he can walk across the sky without falling.

Maybe—just maybe—my Fake Mom is my Real Mom.

But trust me, once everyone has turned their attention back to the goddamn crunchy carrots at dinner, even Fake Mom looks away and snorts into her hand until tears run down her face.

The Sex Talk

So, we've got this guy in middle school now. Joey. Our oldest. And he is all sorts of cool. Savvy. Phrases like *let's play* have been replaced by *let's hang out.* He makes scrambled egg sandwiches for himself in the morning and wants to walk home from the bus stop alone in the afternoon. There is swagger in his neon-sneakered step.

In the spring all the parents of incoming fifth graders were invited to the middle school cafeteria so we could preview The Movie. You know, The Movie that shows ten-year-old kids how their bodies change and mature, what they can expect as they enter puberty and discover the opposite sex.

Let me just say that I learned a few things.

I had always imagined Joe and I would sit our oldest down when the time came and have the Sex Talk. But a while ago I realized he knows way more than we think; juicy details and tidbits gleaned from the back of the school bus and from movies and music. Every once in a while he'll ask something like, "So you and Dad had sex five times?" And I will say, "Yes, just five."

He and I were alone in the car one afternoon, talking

about kids and families, and I asked him how many kids he'd like to have.

"Oh, I don't know," he answered casually. "I guess it depends on how much I enjoy having sex."

I nodded nonchalantly, my eyes trained on the road. I really didn't know what to say.

For most parents, the Sex Talk is probably the "big" one, the one they most dread. But when you've got a kiddo on the spectrum there's another talk to worry about. And I've been dreading this talk, the You Have Autism talk, much more than the Sex Talk.

Because sex—although an awkward and uncomfortable subject—ultimately leads to family and children. Discovering sex is like a flame gathering speed along a long fuse, eventually exploding in a brilliant spark of color and enlightenment.

But discovering you have autism? That's like saying *listen, I know we've been pretending all along that you're just like the rest of us, that it's perfectly normal to ask people when they will die and remember what year Hershey started making chocolate. But it's not. You're not. You are different, diagnosed, identified. You have something called Autism Spectrum Disorder.*

I figured we'd sit Jack down at some point soon and have that discussion, about him and his autism, but for the most part, the You Have Autism Talk seemed to be following the same path as the Sex Talk. In the past year or so, Jack has started picking up on little details here and there that make him different, things like speech therapy and having an aide and stimming.

But instead of a spark igniting, I pictured this discovery

more like a balloon full and buoyant with air. Each new finding—each new *why do I have an aide and Rose doesn't*—is like the tiniest leak, until the brightly colored circle drifts to the floor, empty and weightless. I knew, though, that it wouldn't be too much longer before the balloon deflated.

A lot of people ask me when Jack's three brothers and one sister discovered he had autism, and the truth is that I'm not sure.

Well, that's not exactly true.

I remember very well the day my oldest son Joey came home from school—fresh from chatter on the playground—and asked if I knew Jack had something called autism. He was probably about seven.

Our third son, Charlie, wasn't too far behind. This is probably because Joey and Charlie cannot keep a secret from one another; although three years apart, they are in many ways like one mind. What one knows, the other one learns. It's as if something isn't real until they tell it to each other, usually whispered across the small room they share right before they drift off to sleep.

"Charlie, Charlie. It's called autism. That's why he jumps around and gets upset if there's static on the radio."

As for Rose and Henry, it's really hard to say. Rose certainly knows, but I don't remember a specific day she asked me about it. Rather, her unusual brother has always been a part of her norm; his stimming is the background noise to her day, and his robotic voice is as familiar to her as her own raspy tone.

Somehow she learned the term for his diagnosis, probably from hearing me explain Jack to others when we're out and about at the grocery store and the library, or when she overhears me talking about it on the phone to doctors and teachers.

He has autism. Yes, autism. You know, he's on the spectrum, the autism spectrum.

But as usual, Rose adds her own flair to the expression, and when she says it, it sounds slightly southern and very sweet.

He has the *owt-ism.*

She is watchful of him in the way a mother bird is watchful of her baby chicks. Well, maybe *watchful* isn't the right word. It's more like she's aware of him, attentive and conscious of his moods and temperament.

"Mom, he needs to move right now. He needs to do his zoomies."

These days, they spend a lot of time together: watching television and baking brownies and grocery shopping with me. They play a made-up game they call Hair Salon in her room most days after school, and Jack draws up long, complicated schedules for the salon hours and services: *hair drying from 3:00–3:30, nail polish from 4:00–4:10.*

And Henry? Oh, Henry. Or Henry-Benry, as we sometimes call him. Jack was four years old when Henry was born, and it's as if our youngest child always just knew, in the way the planets know to orbit the sun.

He doesn't yet have a name for it, and if you asked him about his older brother, Henry would probably say, "Oh, he jumps a lot," or "Sometimes he doesn't hear you," giving the impression that Jack is a hearing-impaired grasshopper.

In fact, that is what autism means to Henry at this time;

it means Jack jumps and grunts and stims, and when Henry asks him to put music on or to get him a cookie from the high shelf, he often gets a blank stare until he repeats himself a few times. Loudly.

To me, it's breathtaking the ways in which autism changes everything, and yet it changes nothing for them. He is their brother, and that is all.

They aren't scared for his future or wondering if he'll graduate high school or where he's going to live when he's thirty. Instead, they stand firmly in autism's here and now; how to get Jack to taste clams and check off items on the grocery list.

"Jack, Jack we got the butter. It's in the cart. Cross it out on the paper."

In the end, I believe Joe and I will owe most of Jack's progress to them.

Watching them is like watching a sun with a collection of planets, but sometimes it's difficult to tell who is orbiting whom. Some days the four of them circle Jack watchfully, careful of his heat and weather. Other times, he is drawn to each one of them for sustenance and direction.

And together they warm and change each other, they help one another grow.

My Brother, the Superhero

"Tomorrow morning. At 6:45. I'm going to be on TV," Jack announced through a mouthful of kale. The chatter at the dinner table came to a screeching halt, and we all stared at him.

TV? I thought to myself during the pocket of silence. Didn't you just go to school and come home today? When did you have time to go on TV?

I racked my brain. Maybe I had signed a permission slip at some point and forgotten about it. It's very possible, given the deluge of lunch menus and field trip notices and fundraiser forms I am presented with every day. (And by "presented with" I mean "thrown on the counter along with half-eaten bananas and empty water bottles and rubber band bracelets made from some weird thing called a rainbow loom for me to sift through and sort according to age, grade, and required response.")

"You be on TV?" Henry asked incredulously. "Wif Batman?"

"Jack," Rose asked sweetly, "Did you talk into a microphone? Did you smile for the camera? It's always good to smile."

"Oh, I know what he means," Joey interrupted. "We did the same thing last year. The weatherman from WMUR came in and told everyone in class to wave to the camera." (WMUR carries our local news and the morning weatherman, Kevin Skarupa, makes it a habit of visiting just about every elementary school in New Hampshire.)

"And Batman there too?" Henry asked again, referring to his favorite superhero, his idol, the figure that adorns nearly every t-shirt, every sock, every pair of underwear in my four-year-old's drawer.

"But wait," Rose said with a worried look. "What if Jack, you know, bounces around? Because of his owt-ism?" Charlie added quietly, "Yeah mom. You know, he has a hard time sitting still. What if he had his zoomies?"

"Jack, did you need to zoom while the weatherman was there?"

"NO! I was STILL! I WAVED!"

We all looked over at him, galloping across the kitchen at that very second. Henry leaped up from his seat and joined his brother. Together they bounced the span of the kitchen and family room, back and forth, back and forth.

"See! I jump wike Jack!"

As the youngest, Henry doesn't grasp *different* or *diagnosed* or *Autism Spectrum Disorder*. To him, his older brother is just Jack, just another sibling to pester, to boss, to demand *get me more cookies off the highest shelf in the cabinet.* He's never watched Jack navigate the hallways of elementary school with an aide or hold up the bus with a tantrum. But he does know Jack's the go-to guy for television operation and car identification. "Jack, Jack, what that car behind us? A Toyoya?"

He knows Jack jumps.

Henry does understand, however, that unlike "Jo-Jo" and "Chawlie," Jack will only take so much of a four-year-old's belligerence before retaliating with a low growl or a quick cuff on the shoulder. Like a bear who has been poked too often, Jack has less patience for nonsense.

As a mother of five, I am as attentive to the relationships between my kids as I am to the individuals themselves, and I notice every day how Jack's interactions with all his siblings continue to evolve, continue to show elements of how he's becoming a big brother.

The four boys share a bedroom with two sets of bunk beds, affectionately referred to as the "orphanage," and Rose is on her own in a green- and pink-bedecked room. One evening, just after I had tucked my little flower into bed underneath her monkey quilt and was headed in to settle the boys and turn out their light, I overheard this conversation between eight-year-old Jack and six-year-old Charlie:

Charlie: "I'm scared of the Halloween obstacle course in the gym."

Jack: "I did it. Today. It's not scary. I have gym on Tuesdays."

Charlie: "It's too dark, they shut the lights out."

Jack: "I had gym today. Every Tuesday I have gym. It wasn't too dark."

Charlie: "I'm not doing it."

Jack: "You can. I will go. I will help you."

Charlie: "I don't think I can."

Jack: "I will be there."

I leaned against the door jamb and listened to my two boys exchange these words, and I thought about how Joe and I didn't know if Jack would ever speak in sentences, ever have a full conversation or a meaningful discussion. Hearing him reassure his brother about the dark, his determination to help Charlie enjoy the obstacle course, made me realize just how far our blue-eyed boy has traveled.

And I thought about how, once again, Jack reminded me of autism's beauty, how pure and innocent and genuine his lens to the world is. How he manages to clear away the clutter of life and understand the things that really matter. He doesn't care about *schedules* and *class routines* and *we don't have gym at the same time*. Instead, he cares about things like *family* and *courage* and *loyalty*. He cares deeply about being a brother.

I will help you.

At breakfast the next morning, while the two boys sat at the counter with bowls full of cereal, I tentatively asked Charlie if he would like Jack to help him in gym the following day. "Yes!" he cried enthusiastically.

I will go.

After they left for school I emailed two teachers and one case manager to see if we could somehow have Jack pop into the gym during Charlie's class, explaining how important it was to both of them. The three women coordinated schedules and made adjustments so that, for thirty minutes in the cavernous school gym, a boy with autism could have a chance to be the leader, a chance to teach his younger brown-eyed brother how to play in the dark.

You can.

When they got off the bus I asked Charlie how it went during gym, and he said, "There was only one problem." I asked him what that problem was, a nervous pit in my stomach. Did Jack get upset and throw a tantrum? Did he change his mind at the last minute and refuse to participate?

"We didn't get to go through as many times as I wanted!" he chortled, grinning a wide grin. "It was so fun!" Charlie held my hand as we walked slowly up our long driveway, chatting animatedly about how he and his brother jumped and crawled and ran together, while Jack hovered near us with a small smile playing on his lips.

I will be there.

And he was. I know at this point it's hard to predict what sort of role each of Jack's siblings will play in his adult life once Joe and I are gone. Will they take care of him? Will he live with them and their families, bouncing from brother to sister to brother throughout the years, everyone's "Uncle Jack"? Or will he create a life of his own, a life of independence and children and Toyota Sequoias like Dad drives?

The only certainty about this is the uncertainty.

When I watch my sons ride bikes or work a puzzle together, the biblical story of David and Goliath comes to mind, with Jack the reigning champ for height and weight in our family right now, larger even than ten-year-old Joey.

But although their sizes may suggest David and Goliath, mouse and bear, the dynamic between the brothers is a stark contrast to the battling duo from the Bible. Writing this essay, I grappled to find a story of brotherhood, and like a delicate hummingbird on a bright flower, my mind lighted on Steinbeck's *Of Mice and Men*, the tragic tale of two men—one large and one small, one bright and one so very limited.

I am not ready to reduce my children to a cliché, however, a maxim, a time-worn tale of brawn and brains. It simply does not describe them.

It doesn't describe how Jack first demonstrated empathy by helping a fallen Henry up from the driveway, saying *come on do not cry you will be okay*. Or how Henry grabbed his brother's hand one night in the playroom when they were dancing Gangnam style, his face lit and beaming as they moved to the Korean beat.

It doesn't begin to describe the way Henry can keep Jack's feet firmly planted in our world, booming loudly *look at me I talkin' to you* and *I no want to hear Wady Gaga anymore* and *answer me Jack answer me now*. Because like his older brother, Henry also has little patience for nonsense.

Or how together, they jump.

I returned to my keyboard, to Google, and continued my search. After a few minutes I came across this quote from Marc Brown, children's author and creator of the *Arthur* series:

"Sometimes being a brother is even better than being a superhero."

Yes, I thought to myself. That's it.

Let Jack be the superhero for as long as he can; mighty and strong, tender and compassionate. Let him be the teacher of cars and license plates and music, while simultaneously learning to say *I am sorry you are hurt* and *okay what song do you want to hear next.*

Let him be Batman to the younger Robins.

The next morning Jack was standing over me at exactly 5:59 a.m., already dressed in his stiff new jeans and a blue t-shirt. "Today. At 6:45. We need to watch the news. I will be on TV."

Joe had left for work already. Reluctantly I dragged myself from the warm bed into the chill of the early fall morning. I tied my black robe around my waist and took his hand.

"Okay, Jack. Let's go see." We made our way downstairs into the darkened kitchen, and I turned on the lights and started his favorite breakfast—pancakes—while he perched at the counter and chattered about the weather, about TV, about celebrities.

One by one, three brothers and a sister straggled in sleepily and burrowed into the cushions of our dark red couch. We turned the TV on at 6:40 and sat waiting, waiting to see the segment with Jack's class.

At last—after a weather teaser, the sports coverage, and news about a fire and a local robbery—Kevin Skarupa reappeared, standing against the familiar backdrop of the elementary classroom.

"Where are you?" I asked, squinting at the screen. The camera kept panning quickly back and forth, back and forth across the group of waving kids.

"I don't know," Jack said worriedly. "Maybe I was in the bathroom then."

"Jackie!" Rose squealed, calling him by her special nickname. She pointed to the screen. "There you are! Look! In the corner!"

And there he was, standing in the corner of the room, tentatively waving. Joey and Charlie and Rose jumped off the couch to cheer, to hug, to pat a beaming Jack on the back. Henry sat still, uncharacteristically quiet and seemingly in awe, with his thumb in his mouth and his blue eyes opened wide.

"Jack. You on TV," he whispered reverently. "Just wike Batman."

Thanksgiving Victory

Unless you're talking about football, or scoring the last flat-screen television from Wal-Mart's dusty shelves at midnight, you don't usually hear the words *Thanksgiving* and *victory* in the same sentence. That is, unless you were eating your turkey at *our* house this year.

Joe and I hosted twenty-five people from his family, which meant we needed two turkeys. Which meant we held a contest to see whose turkey came out better.

The day had quite the highlight reel. At breakfast, Jack bellowed, "This is going to be the best Thanksgiving EVER!" We couldn't get him to elaborate *why* it was going to be so great, but we were thankful for his new attitude. Last year he said things like, "Thanksgiving is so STUPID!" and, "When are these people going to LEAVE?"

Whenever we host a holiday, Jack hides from all of his cousins in one of the bedrooms and listens to his music all day. He usually eats with his younger siblings at the kitchen island and bolts back upstairs as soon as he's done. I imagine for a young boy with autism, Thanksgiving resembles one of the circles of hell Dante writes about in his *Inferno*:

hordes of out-of-town guests, people pushing things like shrimp and cheese spread at you all day, the offensive smells of roasted vegetables and turkey brine. So you can see why I was both surprised and pleased by his reaction this time.

In the spirit of competition, Joe and I decided to name our turkeys. I ignored Joe's suggestions of "Runner Up" or "Sore Loser," and settled on Felix. I don't really remember what Joe named his—for the purpose of this story we'll just call it Tasteless.

Around noon I took Felix out of his brine and lovingly patted him down like a newborn fresh from a bubbly bath. I massaged his tender skin with butter and salt and stuffed him with fresh lemon and garlic and rosemary. Joe and I both started cooking our birds at the same time, Felix in the oven and Road Kill on the barbecue rotisserie.

Eventually all of the aunts, uncles, cousins, and grandparents trickled in, and we enjoyed an afternoon of appetizers, cocktails, and fun. Throughout the festivities I checked on Felix, adjusting his tin foil cape and making sure he was basted. At exactly 5 p.m. Joe's beast was done, but Felix's timer stubbornly refused to pop.

While Joe paraded his gaudy gobbler around to enthusiastic *oohs* and *aaahs*, I sent telepathic messages to Felix through the oven door. Pop, bird, pop! Finally, I made a veteran's decision to take my turkey out of the oven. (I don't really know what gave me the courage to do this, seeing as I'm hardly a veteran of turkey-roasting. But I was desperate.)

Dressed in a Batman apron, Joe carved Dried-and-Ugly. His mother gallantly asked for a leg off his turkey, and I loudly assured her she'd eaten her last meal at my table. She smiled widely and pushed her plate closer to accept the meat. Traitor.

I enlisted the help of my sister-in-law, Ann Marie, to carve Felix. She stood at the island working while I stirred the gravy at the stove and hissed mean, un-sisterly things like "Don't butcher him!" and "Do you even know how to carve a turkey?"

At long last, twenty-five Cariello's commenced to the table for the traditional meal. In the midst of all the chaos I heard Jack's robotic voice: "No. I will sit with my cousins. I will move." And, wonder of all wonders, Jack moved his own place setting from the island to sit with his brothers and older cousins at the large table in the family room. We watched in amazement as he smiled and giggled at their jokes and banter.

During dinner our guests declared a tie between Felix and Unsavory. They chuckled good-naturedly and said that both turkeys were delicious; they couldn't possibly pick a winner.

Pansies.

And then, just like that, the meal was over. We rose from the table, groaning over our fullness, and began to clean the kitchen and pack up the leftovers. Ann Marie motioned to me. Silently, she used the silvery tip of my brand-new Cutco knife to point out the place where Felix's plump thigh joined his body. It was purple and shiny. Undercooked.

In that moment Ann Marie's dark eyes bore into mine and a message passed between us. This message stood for sisterhood and loyalty and allegiance. It said *we are now in this together* and *we will take this secret to our graves*. Without a word, I held the large black Hefty bag open and she slid what was left of poor Felix into it. No one was the wiser.

On her way out my mother-in-law grasped my arm with her leather-gloved hand and whispered, "Your turkey was better. Juicier." I smiled benevolently and accepted my praise with dignity and grace; I couldn't bring myself to tell her that in a few short hours she might very well be hunkered over what my Italian father-in-law calls the *terlet bowl*, sick from salmonella poisoning. I wanted to hold on to my victory for as long as I could.

Just then, Jack ran to where we were both standing by the door and shouted, "Grandma. Don't GO. It's not time to leave." Her face opened in surprise and she pulled him into a tight hug.

After that I didn't give Felix another thought. Seeing Jack eat with the other kids and hug his grandmother—hearing him wanting his grandmother to stay—was the only victory any of us really needed.

When Your Grandchild Has Autism

I meet a lot of grandparents when I give readings and talks. During the discussion afterwards they usually ask similar questions, questions like *I have a granddaughter with autism. What should I do when she flaps her hands?* or *Why do the tags on his sweater bother him so much?*

One time I met a tall slender man with thick white hair in Barnes & Noble. He talked to me for almost ten minutes about his twelve-year-old granddaughter's bright blue eyes, her fear of the dark, her obsession with *Teenage Mutant Ninja Turtles*. And then he looked straight at me and asked if I thought she would ever get married.

Whether they go by Grandma and Grandpa, or Nana and Pop, or Meme and Bumpa, they all ask about *sensory integration* and *self-stimulation*, buzzwords that weren't around when they had small children. They are hungry for knowledge and yearn to connect with their sometimes spinning, often silent, grandsons and granddaughters.

I never feel like I have enough time to answer these questions the way I would like, so I stammer and stumble through something meaningless and disjointed.

"Oh, you know! They all develop at their own pace."

Then I pack up the extra books and my black pen and walk to my car feeling unfinished, incomplete.

Back when we were in the midst of Jack's diagnosis, we lived in Buffalo and Joe's parents lived in Lake Carmel—a six-hour drive away. Over the phone every week I would describe Jack's lack of speech, his delay in development, the eerie way he wouldn't look at me. And they always said the same thing: *give it time, his older brother Joey is talking for him, he is fine he is fine he will be fine.*

Jack was nearly three when we moved to New Hampshire, and my in-laws followed from Lake Carmel about a year later. By that point it was well understood that Jack was not fine.

Before long they started taking some of the other kids to sleep at their house, to teach them meatball-making and then sing them to sleep in the small guest room. But not Jack. One time they drove down the driveway with Joey and Charlie waving from the backseat of their Saturn while Jack stood next to me, turning the same Little People figure over and over in his hand. I couldn't help but feel as though some invisible line had been drawn: *them*, but not *him*. They would never understand Jack, never be able to handle him.

And who could blame them? At that time Jack was a total flight risk, adept at picking locks and slipping silently outside. He only knew about a dozen words. He threw giant tantrums and woke several times a night. And the truth was that they were as heartbroken as we were. They longed to connect with their enigmatic grandson, to play checkers and make meatballs and teach woodworking.

I can't say there was a turning point exactly—a lightbulb moment when Grandma and Grandpa at last understood the intricacies of the spectrum disorder and became Autism Whisperers—but I can say they never gave up in their pursuit to understand this sandy-haired boy.

I remember one time when they spent the afternoon at our house during late fall. It was chilly out and we were all outside on the play set, brown leaves crunching underfoot. Except for Jack. He would not leave the house, staying just inside the kitchen, watching everyone through the window like an interloper on the wrong side of the glass.

Every ten minutes or so either Grandma or Grandpa would walk inside to try and coax him outdoors, perhaps to swing high on the swings or slide fast down the slide. I bet they tried at least a dozen times, until at last Jack emerged—wearing neither shoes nor a jacket.

I saw Joe's mother look him over and start to say, "Jack you need a jacket. It's cold . . ." before Joe interrupted, "Let it go, Mom. He's here; he came out."

Finally, when he was about six, it was Jack's turn to spend the night at his grandparents' cozy one-story ranch, his turn to gently drift off as his grandmother sang Italian lullabies in the darkened bedroom. And once he was asleep, Joe's mother and father kept a silent vigil over him all night long—watching and waiting in case he woke up and slipped out the door, even though his days of wandering were behind him.

Jack is older now, and has grown. Sometimes we go to Joe's parents for Sunday dinner, and he will march up to Joe's mother in the middle of the meal with a yellow pear in his hand and wordlessly thrust it at her. Joe and I object and protest: *Jack. Grandma isn't done eating yet; let her finish.* But every time she shushes us and bends closer to him, whispering for him to hand her the ripe fruit. She picks up her knife and peels it, handing him section after section while he hovers at her elbow.

Over the years they have figured one another out. Jack has learned to close the door and Grandpa and Grandma understand that Jack will wear a jacket when he's cold. He stays there regularly.

If I stopped right here, if I told the grandfather at Barnes & Noble this collection of stories, my message would have been obvious and clichéd: When your grandchild has autism you need to accept what you can't change and love them for who they are and never give up and and and and . . .

But it still would have been meaningless and unfinished. Because I have another memory that keeps popping up in my subconscious, a memory that somehow seems important, integral.

We were at my sister-in-law's house just outside of Boston for a birthday party. Jack was about three, and over the course of the afternoon he and two-year-old Charlie were at each other again and again, fighting and kicking. I don't even remember why, but I think it had something to do with a deflating balloon. I vaguely recall them grabbing and snatching and shrieking for it as it drifted around the crowded kitchen.

I do remember I was hot and I do remember I was irritated. I remember I was tired of hearing my two boys screech and scratch at each other, tired of separating them again and again. Finally, Joe put Jack in a timeout in the living room and instructed him to stay there.

Alone, he sat in the other room, screaming and crying as the rest of us shifted nervously in our chairs. Then all at once Joe's mother got up, and walked determinedly over to where Jack sat. She picked him up and cradled him against her shoulder. When Joe protested, she looked up at her six-foot-tall son and said firmly, "Enough. We are done with this."

Both Joe and I were outraged. Outraged that she interfered, outraged with one another, outraged with a son we could not figure out. On the hour-long car ride back to New Hampshire we niggled and argued, bickering about timeouts and in-laws and how to handle children who threw tantrums.

But sitting at my desk now, six years later, I finally understand what my mother-in-law had figured out during that party. She didn't know the terminology for *sensory integration* or *regulation* or *self-stimulation*, but she recognized a small boy who was overwhelmed and tired and sad. She didn't need sophisticated language to diagnose two parents who were on the verge of a breakdown.

I would like to tell all of the grandparents this:

Yes, there are unfamiliar terms like *joint attention* and *individualized education plan* and *theory of mind*, but at the end of the day, it's just you and this child. Do not be afraid. Deep down you already know these phrases; you know when a child has had enough.

When your grandchild has autism, sometimes you'll need to forgo the jacket. You'll need to stay up through the night. You'll need to accept what you can't change and love them for who they are. But when your grandchild has autism, never forget that you have your own message to share and lessons to teach. Sing the lullabies and make the meatballs.

Autism has a lot of heartbreak, but many rewards. These gifts can be hard to see and easy to miss; some days it's just a quick hug goodbye, a mouthful of ziti at dinner, a smile across the table.

Some days, it may look like nothing more than a small boy standing next to you with his palm outstretched, waiting for his slice of a juicy yellow pear.

Making Eye Contact

"You will pick me up at 11:30. 11:30. Pick me up," Jack reminded me in the morning as he hopped from one foot to the other. "And after my appointment we will go to Bertucci's in the mall. For lunch."

I asked him to have a seat and finish the giant bowl of cereal he'd poured for himself, and then I promised I would be at the school on time to pick him up for his annual appointment with the eye doctor.

"The doctor. He needs to check my eyes."

Like many things about Jack, his eyes are peculiar; as a toddler he was diagnosed with Horner's Syndrome, where one pupil is almost always dilated larger than the other. Harmless, but a little weird.

In first grade his teacher, the lovely Mrs. Cushman, noted that he looks down at the paper with his head tilted to the right and reads from the outside corner of his eye. Once she pointed it out, I began to notice how often he slants his head that way; whether choosing a cookie from a plate or playing the Wii, Jack tends to position himself so he peers from his right eye.

We started taking him to the optometrist, and although Jack had a hard time staying regulated and still for the exam, he managed—in between shrieks—to spit back a few letters from the eye chart. We figured the head-tilting was just another one of his quirks, no different from the way he rolls pancakes between his fingers or clears his throat loudly three dozen times a day.

At nine, his one eye continues to have a larger black center than the other, and he still reads from the corner of his right eyeball. But, really, the most notable thing about his vision this year is that he's started to make regular eye contact, to connect his gaze with ours when he's speaking.

We also realized earlier this year that Joey needed glasses, so on Wednesday I figured it was possible we'd leave the doctor's office with a prescription for Jack's lenses, genetics being what it is. I knew, if we did, that I would have to remind Jack ninety million times to find, clean, and wear them—just like I do for his older brother.

This year Jack was calmer as we walked into the optometrist's busy reception area. Although stimming quite a bit, he happily climbed into the seat and started to ask a bajillion questions about the blood pressure band, whether there are scorpions in New Hampshire, how long it takes to drive to Oklahoma.

Once the doctor came in, Jack sat up straighter, placed the plastic shield over his left eye, and began to read the chart in his robotic voice. "A V P D E are there black widow spiders in the woods S T R X have you ever seen a South Dakota license plate?"

Wow, I thought to myself. What a difference a year makes.

Then it was time to cover the right eye. "I CAN'T!" he cried, twisting and turning in the gray leather exam chair. "I need my OTHER EYE to see it!"

"Jack, just use your left eye and read the letters," the doctor gently encouraged.

"I CANNOT! I can't see them. Please. I need my eye. My OTHER eye," he begged.

"Jack," I admonished him quietly from where I perched on the edge of a chair in the corner, a sick feeling washing over me. "Do not fool around. Can you see these letters?"

"No! Stop asking!"

I kept my own eyes firmly locked on the screen as the doctor enlarged the size of the capital "A" until it was several inches high, and with each increase my stomach sank lower and lower. I covered my mouth with my hand.

"We won't know for sure until he sees a pediatric specialist, but at best he's legally blind in his left eye," the doctor said softly.

He went on to explain that Jack basically had an exaggerated version of something called a lazy eye. His right eye has been doing all the work for the left, and the left had grown weaker and weaker until finally losing most of its vision. I had a lazy eye myself as a little girl, and I remember having to wear an eye patch in kindergarten. To this day I can call to mind the sensation of tears puddling in the bottom of the sticky patch as I begged my mother to take it off before school. I wore it for a few months, though, and it worked. My eye strengthened.

"Hopefully," the doctor went on, "the vision isn't too far gone, and we can improve it by blurring or covering his right eye."

Too far gone?

I struggled to explain. He doesn't bump into things. He never drops a book or spills his milk or so much as knocks a fork off the table when he stims at dinner. He was the first in our house to master riding a bike without training wheels and when you look at him, his eyes track together—two blue orbs that light up my heart when they occasionally meet mine.

Legally blind?

"He's adapted," the doctor reminded me. "I have adults who come in here and don't realize one eye has grown stronger than the other. He'll continue to adapt if he has to."

Adapt, I thought bitterly. Yes, Jack is no stranger to adapting. Every single day my son wakes up and adapts his rigid mind to a world full of fire drills and barking dogs and standardized testing, where people picture Tuesday in tones of black and white and grey, while his weeks explode with color. A world that demands flexibility, where he hears me say that *oh yes you will try that chicken pot pie*.

With the phrase *legally blind legally blind legally blind* bouncing around my brain, I struggled to keep my composure as we left the office. Once we were in the car I quickly called Joe, while Jack shouted from the third row.

"94.1 please. I need 94.1. And Bertucci's for LUNCH! Bertucci's and 94.1!"

A tremendous wave of guilt washed over me. Those words—*legally blind*—began to weave themselves together with the phrase *my fault my fault my fault*. This is *my fault*. Why didn't I take him to get his eyes examined more often than once a year? Why didn't I push harder to understand the head-tilting?

So many times I'd notice him reading his homework out of the corner of his right eye and I would ask him why, why he looked at the page that way, and he'd answer, "Because. I do," or "I like this way."

I know vision loss is difficult to self-diagnose; Joey's need for eyewear snuck up on us, and Joe and I exchanged wary, guilty glances when our ten-year-old tried his glasses on for the first time in the back of the car and exclaimed, "Wow! Was the world always this clear?"

And I know the condition of *legally blind* isn't really all that big a deal; with an acuity of 20/1600, I myself am considered legally blind. As a few of my friends pointed out, many, many people walk around with poor vision in both eyes; corrective eyewear and laser surgery and contact lenses have come a long way.

But sitting in the darkened Bertucci's I considered how, once again, I'd failed to heed my own message: Always understand behavior has meaning. All this time, ever since he was a smaller version of himself wearing his favorite striped blue shirt to first grade, Jack's been turning his head to peer out of the corner of his right eye because his left was slowly clouding, blurring, darkening. How many essays and chapters and articles have I written about autism with the phrase *Jack sees the world through a different lens*? Little did I know how different that lens actually is; for years he's been learning to read and ride a bike and download iTunes through a singular view, and I never knew it.

Am I failing him?

As we walked out of the mall and into the bright afternoon sunlight, Jack squeezed my arm and pointed. "Look. Tennessee. Over there on the Dodge Neon." I looked away, wiped a tear from my own eye, and in an unsteady voice answered him *yes I see Jack-a-boo I see it.*

I see it.

Will I Always Have It?

It was a Sunday morning in late September—the day after my birthday. I was fuzzily turning pancakes on the griddle while Jack perched at the counter flicking the top to the syrup open and closed and open and closed. I was just about to tell him to *stop doing that, it's gross to put your hands all over the lid* when he asked, "Why was I born with autism?"

Quickly, Joe and I shushed the other four and motioned for quiet, because both Joe and I knew our time with his open mind was short, that we had just a precious few moments before the steel trap in his brain snapped shut and moved on to how old Rosa Parks was when she died.

"Well, Jack, it's a part of you, just like your eyes are blue and you have big feet."

"Do all people with blue eyes have it?"

"No, it's not really about your eyes. It's like how you learn things."

And then, in rapid fire, these questions:

"Do grown-ups have it?"

"Who else has it?"

"Will I always have autism?"

"Where did I get it?"

Standing before Jack in our kitchen I briefly wished we were having the Sex Talk instead—I longed for the concreteness of *fallopian tubes* and *ovaries* and *this is how babies are made*.

I mean, how do I tell my nine-year-old that I love his autism but I also hate it and it's beautiful but sometimes it's so very, very ugly?

How do I tell him there are days I literally want to pull my hair out by the handfuls or, better yet, light my eyelashes on fire and run into the street screaming *just measure the effing polygon so we can be done with homework*, that time and time again I am brought to my knees with frustration, with heartache, with fear?

Or how anxiety—a sneaky sidekick to his Autism Spectrum Disorder—came in one February like a thief in the night, threatening to steal his joy, his happiness, the very smile on his face? And how the teeny-tiny white pill he swallows before bed keeps the thief at bay, keeps the occasional giggle in his voice?

How his father and I are constantly sifting through the flood of information and advice about *hyperbaric chambers* and *gluten-free pretzels* and *advanced behavior therapy*, sifting and sorting to concentrate on the brown-haired boy beneath the diagnosis?

But that I can't imagine him without it, without the beauty and wonder and color it adds to our world and our family?

That Sunday night I knelt next to his bed where he was sleeping with beloved Bunny on the pillow. His weighted blanket was pulled to his ears, his blue-rimmed glasses placed carefully on the shelf above him. In the quiet room I started to whisper. I said something like this:

> *Jack, your autism is great. It is not something to be embarrassed about or that you should want to change about yourself. I love it. I mean, we all love it. It's so interesting the way you see the world. I can't wait to know more about it from you. I love you no matter what, I hope you know that.*

But we weren't done yet.

Two weeks later we were having dinner at Shorty's, our local Mexican restaurant. Our meals had just arrived, and in the midst of napkins and salsa and tipping cups, a robotic voice:

"I don't want this autism anymore. I don't want it in me."

I just didn't know what to say. Sitting in a booth at a Mexican restaurant and hearing my son say he wants to rid himself of something that is so fundamentally his, well, it broke my heart wide open.

As it turns out, we didn't have to say anything. His ten-year-old brother did it for us.

Joey turned to his younger brother and, with a mouthful of buffalo chicken burrito he'd ordered off the adult menu, told him, "Jack. I think you're better with it."

"Yeah," Jack said thoughtfully, his own mouth full of corn dog. "Maybe." He glanced over at Joey, and behind the thick lenses of his glasses I glimpsed the smallest spark in his blue eyes.

That night I knelt next to Jack's bed once again and whispered to my sleeping boy:

"You are better with it."

I thought for a second more, and whispered:

"We are better with it."

The Elephant in the Room

Sometimes people write to me and ask questions. They ask me about *anxiety* and *medication* and *social stories* and *good ideas for sidestepping tantrums.*

Although I never feel like I have any good advice to give, I love reading about people's families and hearing their stories of autism and spectrum disorder. I also love it because it gives me a chance to announce to my family that I am working and must be left very, very much alone. Then I flounce into our tiny home office and shut the door. Firing up my laptop, I promptly log on to Facebook or Amazon.

Once I've ordered the skirt and downloaded the book and researched inane trivia like whether or not cats can swim (they can, they just don't like to), I turn back to my email and craft my responses. In order to hide how confused I am myself about autism, I start my answer with really smart-sounding words. It usually goes something like this:

As you know, autism unfolds differently for every individual.

See? SMART.

Last Saturday, I checked email and read this message:

Dear Carrie,

I need help telling my son he is on the spectrum. He is ten and has no idea. We are not sure how to proceed. I wondered if you had written anything you might direct me to regarding telling your son. I would appreciate it so very much.

You might like this: Today is my birthday, and as his gift for my "special day" my son is going to allow me to sing! He promises not to cover his ears and scream . . . for one day. But you know what? I think I will refrain.

Sincerely,

Kim

Ha! So easy! I had already drafted a story about how we tell Jack he has autism, how we compare it to telling my older son about how babies are made—both tricky subjects without exact timetables.

My fingers hovered over the keyboard, ready to copy and paste, then send it along to Kim. Maybe I would even add a quick *Happy Birthday, Kim!* to personalize it a little!

At some point late last summer, Jack began to connect the dots. He started to look around our family and realized he was the only one going to summer school, the only one with an aide, the only one who needed to get up from the dinner table to jump around.

I pictured long, enlightening conversations about self-stimulation and license plates and why he takes a little white pill before bed every night. Do not ask me why I pictured this even as I knew that I've never had a long conversation with this child in my life. Few have been particularly enlightening, either. Mostly, they center around which day we should have pancakes and when toilet paper was invented.

Nonetheless, I was ready. I was excited to finally name the elephant in the room and hear Jack's side of the spectrum story.

Elephant, thy name is autism.

But on the morning we launched into the conversation it did not go as planned. As hard as Joe and I tried to point out the elephant's most interesting qualities, his beautiful silky skin and unfailing memory, Jack wasn't buying it. He could not see what we see. He did not want the elephant.

In fact, he said, "I do not want it. I want it out of me."

Did we tell him too soon? It certainly felt like the right time. I mean, you can only pretend to ignore your son for so long when he asks why he has to go back to school in July while his three brothers and one sister get to swim at the town pool. And we wanted him to hear it from us first.

Would I have changed the way we told him? I don't think so. We were home, in a quiet space. We answered his questions honestly and carefully. We assured him he was loved, and that he was the same little boy he was before.

Textbook, really.

So why do I have a pit in my stomach when I remember our conversation, and all the subsequent exchanges with Jack about autism? Why is it something I struggle with over and over, even though it's now part of our history, another piece of our puzzle?

It's because Jack hates it about himself. He is embarrassed

and afraid and ashamed and confused. And this is heartbreaking. Just last week I had this conversation with Jack:

"I do not want. To go. No summer school."

"Jack, I know, but you have . . ."

"Is it because I'm bad?"

"No, of course not . . ."

"Is it because of autism."

"Not exactly. It's more complicated than that."

"Is it because I didn't pay attention all year when it was math."

"Well, KIND OF!"

Jack never used to mind summer school. When he was younger I just loaded him on the bus, excited to enjoy a couple of hours without having to worry if he was trying to start the car or investigate the toilet.

There is a price to this knowing, tendered in the currency of *I am the only one in my family who goes to summer school* and *why doesn't Charlie have an aide*.

Imagine someone telling you that you've got this condition—this diagnosis—and it's not your fault and you're not sick or anything and there's nothing really wrong with you. But the hot days of summer will be punctuated by the hum of a classroom. You will need someone to escort you to the bathroom in middle school. And for your whole life people may or may not judge you.

There is probably never a good time to hear *you are different from us*.

I am beginning now to glimpse the war that wages within my boy, his fight to push the elephant back to his corner and get rid of something so fundamentally his. I am grateful for his spirit, but some days I just wish I knew which side of the battlefield to take.

Shortly after we told Jack about his autism, my friend Audrey and I went to hear author Daniel Smith speak about his book, *Monkey Mind: A Memoir of Anxiety*. Standing before the audience in the tiny crowded bookstore, he explained how his mother named the anxiety for him at an early age. It made the concept of himself less limber, less flexible. From that point forward he felt tied to the label *anxious*.

Sitting on the folding chair in the front of the room it dawned on me that maybe, by naming *autism*, we had boxed Jack in. We made him less limber. Although we gave him the information, there is nothing he can do about it. Just knowing he has autism doesn't mean he will at once start being flexible or stop stimming or gobble up slimy yogurt.

I imagine it's like dropping the cutest little kitty-cat into a lake and asking him to swim across to the shore beyond. He would hate it. He would screech and flail and complain. With big kitty eyes, he would beg you to carry him to dry land, where he felt safe.

But then I thought about the defiant Jack with his clipped speech: *Big bus big bus like Joey.* I chuckled remembering the first time Jack tried clams casino in a little seafood restaurant outside of Portsmouth. And it occurred to me: maybe I should worry less about where to stand on the battlefield and just get the hell out of his way.

Jack is a fighter, and he will keep on fighting to make his own way in the world, to cross between the shores of autism and not-autism. Who knows? Maybe he'll kick his toes up and float buoyantly on his back somewhere in the middle of that great, vast lake.

Because it's true that cats don't like the water, but elephants are excellent swimmers.

Dear Kim,

As you know, autism unfolds differently for every individual.

All I can say is, you'll know the right time to tell your beautiful son about his diagnosis. And the right time will also feel wrong and then right again and wrong once more.

Okay, basically, there is no right time.

Some days it may feel like there are three of you standing in the room together: you, your son, and a giant elephant lurking in the corner. At times, you may all stagger under the tremendous weight of I am different but I want to be the same, show me how to be the same.

This will hurt.

In fact, your heart will feel like it is breaking into ninety million pieces and it will be hard to breathe.

But ultimately autism is his to own. He alone will bring it out into the light, examine it and unravel it, make sense of it and make peace with it. Do not underestimate his strength.

In the meantime, I only have one piece of advice. Sing.

Sing and screech and yowl like a cat. It's the best way to coax the quiet elephant into the water for a long, cool swim.

Best,

Carrie

Part Two: Community

When Jack was first diagnosed with autism, my inclination was to hold him close to me.

Although I have never once concealed his diagnosis from a single person, never hid his autism or kept it a secret, in many ways I positioned myself as his mediator. This was not exactly a conscious decision—since he was an infant I've had to translate, interpret, decode for him and for those around him: *he wants a cookie* and *the music is too loud* and *Jack wave goodbye wave you can do it wave.*

I guess you could say I was reluctant to release my little fish, to let him swim in the deeper waters beyond our family because I was afraid of how people would react to him. Would the cashier in the Walgreens find him rude? Would the server in Bertucci's understand that Jack is asking for milk, and will the teachers in preschool remember to warn him about the fire drill?

I doubted our community.

I longed for Buffalo, where Jack was born and diagnosed

and somewhat understood. We lived on a beautiful tree-lined street and we walked everywhere because there were sidewalks. There was an adorable bagel shop around the corner we used to go for coffee on Saturday mornings.

It was a great community.

It's so easy to bandy that expression around, isn't it? Oh, what a great community! We love the community! But what does *community* really mean? Technically it means a neighborhood, a group of people. Decent schools and a low crime rate. You can find those things in a lot of places.

But the Buffalo community was more than that, and I can sum it up perfectly with my memory of a November evening eight years ago.

Our oldest, Joey, was three years old. Jack was two, and Charlie just eight weeks. (Rose was a French Martini waiting for us in the distant future, and Henry merely a gleam in the eye of an unreliable urologist.)

Infant Charlie had come down with an ear infection, and for two nights he had howled from the piercing pain. That afternoon the pediatrician had put him on an antibiotic and for most of the evening he seemed listless, lethargic. I remember him raising his tiny hands and sort of swiping at his eyes. When I took him up for his bath, something about the way he moved and whined as I undressed him made me uneasy.

Holding him with just his diaper on, I walked downstairs and told Joe, "Something is wrong. He doesn't look right to me." Sure enough, in the bright light of the living room I saw what I hadn't noticed in the dim light of the bathroom;

Charlie's entire body was covered in hives. All I could think was that he looked like a pineapple.

"Call 9-1-1; he's having a reaction to the antibiotic," Joe commanded, taking Charlie into his arms.

Five minutes later the house was filled with burly EMTs, men wearing white shirts and navy pants and big, heavy work boots. One stood in the corner of the dining room cradling Charlie in his arms and saying weird words like *Epipen* and *anaphylactic* while I felt my own throat close with panic. Joey stood silently by my side, watchful.

Two-year-old Jack had just been diagnosed with autism and, with his own silent agenda, kept walking up to the EMTs and grabbing their hands, trying to lead them to the canister of cookies we kept in the kitchen.

After a moment that felt like forever, it was decided that an ambulance ride to the emergency room was in order. I raced through the house grabbing clothes for the baby and a jacket for myself, while Joe scrambled to look up the babysitter's number so he could meet me at the hospital.

Cradling Charlie in my arms, I flung open the front door and blinked. On our front lawn stood nearly three dozen neighbors. In the dusky light they appeared motionless, until Mr. Simon—the attorney from down the street who walked his little dog Boots past our house every morning—stepped forward and broke the silence.

"What happened? What do you need?"

All at once there was a tumble of words and hugs and hands on our shoulders. One of the EMTs strapped little Charlie to a big stretcher and loaded him into the ambulance while people reassured us with *it's going to be fine we'll stay with the kids you both go.*

That is what the community in Buffalo looked like; a group of neighbors waiting on the front lawn in the chilly November air, waiting to hear why the ambulance was there, if everyone was okay, if there was anything they could do to help.

Less than two years later, we moved to New Hampshire. And it was an adjustment.

There are no sidewalks. No cute bagel shops just around the corner, ready with Saturday morning's coffee. The houses are more spread out, and I can go weeks without seeing my neighbors, especially in the winter. The community certainly felt different from the one we left in Buffalo.

But we settled in and got Jack situated at his new preschool. We had our daughter, Rose, and accidentally had our last son, Henry. We joined Little League teams and karate classes and book clubs and poker groups. We went to church and to the local gym.

Before long, the community in Bedford began to bloom like dogwoods in spring—slow to blossom but brilliant in color.

Despite a close circle of friends and play dates and school activities, nothing quite captured the feeling I experienced that evening in Buffalo, the feeling that we were held together by more than just carpooling and coat drives, potluck dinners and monthly card games.

Until last spring, when we discovered the depth of Jack's vision problems.

Joe and I were reeling, guilty and frustrated. Though

we'd noticed Jack's quirky habit of reading with a tilt that favored his right eye, we'd never investigated his habit more seriously. Combined with his autism, it seemed like just one more challenge Jack would have to overcome.

Someone else was also reeling: Jack. The pediatric ophthalmologist said our autistic son needed to wear a patch over his right eye for two hours a day (to strengthen the left); she also prescribed glasses.

On our way home from a very long afternoon at Children's Hospital, Joe suggested we stop at the optometrist and have Jack pick out his new glasses.

"No! NO STOPPING!"

Quietly, Joe and I agreed to let it go for the night, to just let Jack relax and process the idea of eyewear.

And boy, did he process. Once we got home he raged and stormed and cried about the injustice of glasses. Oh, the glasses. For six hours, this boy fumed and seethed and shrieked and cried over those glasses. We even enlisted ten-year-old Joey. "Jack, Jack you will love it. You will see better," Joey told his hysterical brother, using the shortened speech pattern he learned long ago to get his point across. No luck.

That evening we put Jack to bed, and when I went in to kiss him goodnight, he pulled his weighted blanket up to his chin and chanted tearfully, "No glasses. No glasses. I just want to be normal. Normal."

I wandered back downstairs feeling despondent and hopeless like I always do after one of Jack's marathon tantrums. I emailed his Riddle Brook Elementary School teacher to update her on the situation, and explained to her Jack's resistance to glasses.

Anxious and restless, I hopped on Facebook, and I saw this message she posted just minutes after reading my email: "Riddle Brook friends. . . . please wear glasses tomorrow if you don't regularly do so. It is for a great kiddo who might need some encouragement as he faces a new zig in his zag."

And my heart soared.

By 6:15 the next morning, Jack was standing over my bed chanting, "No glasses. No glasses. I will not wear GLASSES!" I said little in response, merely getting up to prepare breakfast for my kids.

As Jack munched his Cheerios, I told him I thought the teachers had something funny planned, something to cheer him up. But he just griped. "I am not going to school today EITHER," he insisted. Grumpily he trundled to the bus and stomped up the steps without a look back.

All day, as I ran to the supermarket and picked up dry cleaning and bought stamps, I thought about Jack, worried he was lost to his inner world, anguished over eyewear. But just as the bus pulled up I checked email on my phone and saw a picture from his teacher. In it were nearly forty people squeezed into a single frame: teachers, parents, aides, administrators—even a few students. All of them stared into the camera's lens with wide smiles on their faces, a sea of color and hairstyles and expressions. In the background, just on the far wall, you could see a small sign that said "Welcome," a perfect announcement for what seemed like a kind of group hug. But that wasn't the best part.

All of them were wearing glasses.

There were pink ones and tortoise shell ones and metal-framed ones. One person wore safety goggles, another reading glasses. Still another formed her thumbs and first fingers into circles and held these pretend-glasses up to her face. And in the middle of the group, sat Jack, looking slightly astonished, but clearly happy.

When Jack got off the bus at the end of the day, he slumped into his seat in our minivan. "Okay, okay, okay," he said, holding his tattered red backpack on his lap, "I will try my best. With these glasses." And off we went to the optometrist's, where he picked out electric-blue spectacles without any prompting at all.

It took a group of teachers dusting off their glasses to help my son find his way through a new transition, to show him they understand him, they embrace him, they accept him and his autism.

They helped my unusual boy feel normal, even if just for a little while.

This is community.

Now, when I see the cashier in Walgreens smile and hand Jack his bag, when I look at the picture of teachers who wear glasses, I know I am ready to let Jack go, out into the cool, deep pond—the wide, wavy blue world out there.

I Can

"Sometimes. I call Mr. Hines 'Mr. Clean.' "

"Jack! That isn't very nice. He's your teacher."

We were standing in the cleaning aisle of Hannaford's picking up Windex.

"It's a joke. I was making a joke."

I watched him push his glasses up the bridge of his nose, and I noticed the glint in his eye, the quick grin that flashed across his face.

"Huh," I said, pushing the cart forward. "Well, okay. Let's go pick out some ice cream."

Jokes do not always come easily for Jack, but by the fourth grade he understood comedy a little better, and he also learned to tell a few jokes here and there. Progress, right? Yes, but as usual, autism stepped in and blurred the victory.

Indeed, Jack loves to tell jokes, regardless of how funny they might be (or might not be), and whether or not you've heard it before. If he likes it, he'll just tell it over. Over and over. And over. Without any consideration of his audience or how annoying they might find it. He's oblivious to the,

"It's not funny when you say it eleven times" or "Enough, Jack!"

In other words, he can be a Mr. Tells-A-Joke-Too-Much.

You know the type. The guy who tells a knock-knock joke thirty times in a row or the server at the restaurant who booms out, "I can't believe you ATE THE WHOLE THING! Hahahah! You were very hungry!"

And now, Mr. Tells-A-Joke-Too-Much was unleashing his funny on Mr. Hines.

Mr. Hines teaches fourth grade. He is also the head coach for the high school football team, the Bedford Bulldogs. In his class, the kids sit on yoga balls instead of chairs. He is considered the coolest of the cool when it comes to teachers. And yes, he is bald like Mr. Clean. But in a good way. And, oh, how Jack tormented this man all year.

Once a week Mr. Hines put a quote on the board—generally something positive and motivating—and students were supposed to copy it down in their notebooks and write about what it means to them. He expected insightful, creative responses, pretty much the opposite of Jack's answers.

Here are some examples:

August 28: "*Just do it.*"

To which Jack replied, "To me, this quote makes me fall asleep."

September 8: "*No one is useless in the world who lightens the burden of it for anyone else.*"

And Jack's response was, "To me, this quote means take me out of this school it's boring."

Or, this charmer from about halfway through the year:

"The weak can never forgive. Forgiveness is the attribute of the strong."

And Jack's quip this time? "To me, this quote means I need to exercise."

But frankly, the quotes paled in comparison to Mr. Hines' "I Can" campaign.

Jack's not exactly known for his positive attitude or his can-do spirit. He's a little on the negative side, to be honest, and Mr. Hines, being an upbeat and optimistic person, started to challenge Jack's way of thinking by countering him with the phrase "I Can" whenever Jack whined, "I can't."

Which, I imagine, was about a bajillion times a day.

Before long, "I Can" took on a life of its own and the whole class was in on it. There was banter, and the kids even formed teams of "I Can" vs. "I Can't." Jack, remaining stubborn however, made lists on the back of his homework folder and added an apostrophe and a "t" whenever Mr. Hines wrote "I can" on his spelling list or math sheet.

I wasn't crazy about the whole thing. I was afraid Mr. Tells-A-Joke-Too-Much had reared his unfunny head again, and I also thought everyone—Jack included—was missing the point. The purpose behind Mr. Hines' "I Can" was to inspire and motivate, to encourage and support. It was not so the class could divide into teams with half of them chanting "I can't."

But then I noticed something. By late November, the phrase began showing up regularly in Jack's own speech.

"I can stir the pancakes."

"I can go down the driveway on my bike."

"Let me try. I can do it."

I also noticed something else. For the first time ever, Jack began mentioning kids in his class, to name them during dinner or when we were running errands. He even used the word *friend*, as in "My friend Claire loves to say 'I can't' with me." He was connecting, he was building, he was engaging. Even more than that, he was *leading*.

You know, all the things people with autism are not expected to do.

A few weeks before school ended, Mr. Hines sent the quote books home for good. I stood in the kitchen, chuckling over Jack's entries; the messy handwriting and the misspelled words and the attempts at humor. But one from early January struck me:

"*I am.*"

And Jack had written: "I am who I am."

It's not exactly the most creative or original thought in the world. Basically, he just tacked on three extra words to the quote. But it lingered in the back of my mind for a few days.

I am who I am.

I asked him about it when he was playing outside one afternoon.

"I am me. I am good and I can," he said matter-of-factly.

"But those quotes. They stinked," he smirked as he took off down the long driveway on his bike.

Watching him sail downhill, I felt like celebrating. I wanted to celebrate *humor* and *quotes* and *yoga balls* and *fourth grade*.

But more than that, I wanted to celebrate this teacher for

showing my son the power of two tiny words—four letters total—and how they can change his world. For tolerating Mr. Tells-A-Joke-Too-Much long enough to reveal the boy underneath; the boy who is grateful to make a friend and be a friend and share a laugh. The boy who has autism, but does not want to be stuck with it.

The boy who can. I wanted to say all of this, and I thought about writing it in a nice note with my favorite felt-tipped pen. But it seemed as though a thank-you card wouldn't have been quite enough. It wouldn't have done the year justice.

Jack agreed. And so, in the end, we decided on red t-shirts, brightly blazoned with the words "I can!" in white, one for every person in Jack's class—including "Mr. Clean."

I've never seen Jack's smile so wide.

What's Normal?

Nearly every day someone asks me something like, "When did you know that Jack wasn't normal?" Then they stop themselves, stammer a bit, and apologize for saying *normal*. Their faces get all red and they look away and stare at their feet. "I mean, you know, what's *normal*, there is no *normal*, sorry for saying *normal*."

I can never understand what all the fuss is about. Personally, I love the word *normal*. Normal is good. Normal is, you know, normal. If we didn't have normal, we wouldn't have other things like extraordinary or mediocre or stupendous. Normal sets the bar.

For the most part I'm normal. I'm extraordinary at some things (making chocolate-chip banana bread) and mediocre at others (doing pull-ups). I'm not particularly stupendous at anything, so I feel like this balances me out to right around normal. It's a pretty good place to be.

And the rest of my family? Pretty normal. They're a quirky bunch for sure, but the quirky things like Henry's rigidity and Joey's fascination with Minecraft and Charlie's anxiety about thunderstorms are balanced out by all of the other things they're amazing at, like dancing to *Thrift Shop* and throwing a baseball and coloring inside the lines. And making their brother Jack laugh.

Because Jack is not so normal. Jack does not laugh every day (or even every other day). He does not like baseball (or team sports in general), nor does he often play with other kids. He doesn't look people in the eye. He won't eat wet food and he's still terrified of dogs, blue water in the toilet bowl, and fire drills.

It needs to be said and as his mother I have to be the one to say it. I have to own this about him and his autism. He is not normal. It is not normal to ask the same question about black widow spiders a hundred times a day or to shriek if a dog comes on *America's Funniest Home Videos* or to panic if the right radio station isn't playing in the car.

But you know what else is not normal about Jack?

The uncanny way he remembers dates.

His love of music.

His ability to operate appliances.

Last year, my sister's son made his First Communion, and in the middle of the party afterwards Jack was dereg-ulated and distressed and excited. He was bouncing from room to room, making his way around the guests as he stimmed and zoomed. Every once in a while he would take his fingers out of his mouth long enough to screech at my sister, begging her to make sure her dogs were not going to break loose. Sarah, good aunt that she is, took this all in stride and soothed him by saying the dogs were away, he was safe, not to worry. I, terrible mother that I am, barely noticed, mostly because this is how Jack is every time we visit my sister and I'm used to him. Also because she had the best chocolate cake with sugary white frosting I've ever tasted, so I was distracted.

At one point I stood balancing my second slice of cake and chatting with a guest who pointed out how normal Jack seemed, how high-functioning he was. I looked over at my son, who just then had leaped on top of my brother-in-law's eighty-year-old, five-foot-tall, a-hundred-pounds-soaking-wet Italian uncle's back because he thought he heard one of the dogs coming up the stairs. I set my cake down, and walked over, apologizing to Uncle Joey and untangling my nine-year-old's legs from the stunned man's bony hips.

Yep, that's really normal.

I understand that it's a natural instinct to try and fit Jack into the mold of ordinary, regular, typical. To normalize him. I tried to do it myself in the early days, when I was a terrified new mother and he a wordless toddler. But slowly I'm learning how counter-productive it is to shove a square Jack into our round world, how heartbreaking and painful and wrong it feels.

Over the winter we were stuck in the house on a snowy Sunday afternoon. When we finished lunch I told the kids they needed to find something productive to do, that the television and Wii were finished for the day. (And, yes, The Great Wii Tirade did eventually end and they got it back. But I still manage it pretty carefully.)

After a lot of groaning and negotiating, they all headed off in different directions: Joey to his Lego table, Charlie and Rose to a game of chess, and Henry to his jigsaw puzzle of the United States. Meanwhile, Jack pulled out a long-forgotten Christmas gift, a calendar-making kit.

I wandered into the kitchen where he was coloring and stopped to admire his work. I was touched to notice he'd included all of our birthdays and had drawn a picture of each person, along with their favorite gift for that particular month. In that moment I had an odd thought. Sitting at the kitchen counter, watching him painstakingly draw a Lego brick for Joey in March, I thought, *I am so glad we understand his diagnosis.*

If Jack didn't have a diagnosis, if we went along trying to pretend he was all fine and normal even when we knew deep down that he wasn't, I would not have been sitting in my warm kitchen praising his project on that wintry day. I would be stressed out, wondering why he doesn't color in the lines, why he is always playing alone, why he doesn't answer me right away when I ask him what his favorite color is.

I would spend all of my time concentrating on what he is not, rather than what he is.

This doesn't mean I've lowered the bar for him—quite the opposite. Jack's diagnosis motivates me to constantly figure out how to help him be the best version of himself he can possibly be. But that version may never really be normal, and that's just fine with me.

Because I don't want normal. Normal won't tell me that Thursday is red and what movie we saw on February 22nd, 2013. Normal won't inspire me to look for the Wyoming license plate.

Maybe you're wondering how the rest of the day went at my sister's house. Eventually Jack settled down, and Joe hoisted him on his back and took him down to the basement to peer into the room where the dogs were staying. While Joe calmly pointed out how gentle the dogs were, Jack alternated between covering his ears and clinging to his father's shoulders. But he stayed there, quieting down just long enough to look closely and say *they look tired today*.

May the Smallest Wolf Tame a Mighty Snake

"Oh, you're so good with her! I bet you'd love a dog of your own," said the woman sitting on the bleachers.

Joey looked up from where he and Charlie stood petting a shaggy Golden Retriever, and cheerfully answered, "Oh, we can't. My brother Jack's afraid of them."

"Yeah, he's really scared," Charlie chimed in with a rueful smile.

It's no secret that Jack's been terrified of dogs since he was about two years old. I devoted an entire chapter of my first book to the dog problem, and I know that those of you who have read it all had a good, long laugh at me when you got to the part where I screamed at an elderly blind man to get his service dog out of the way. But that's okay. I forgive you. I'm really kind and generous that way.

There have been small breakthroughs, of course. One time Jack petted a dog in the hotel lobby of a Hampton Inn, surprising us all. Last summer he reached out a finger and stroked my friend Pam's new puppy. But for the most part, he's still very afraid.

This is stressful, the dog thing. It means if we're going to someone's house for dinner I have to call and diplomatically ask what the plans are for the family pet so I can prepare Jack. Typically, we would use a social story, or a visual set of pictures, to help Jack understand the places in the house where the dog will be, and where he can go for a quiet break.

The last time it was my sister-in-law's turn to host Thanksgiving, it was quite a show, let me tell you. She has two dogs, and Jack started whimpering before we even parked the car. In between bites of turkey and mashed potatoes, Joe and I spent the entire meal telling him to calm down and stop screaming, trying to get him to finish his dinner before he fled to the basement because the dogs didn't go down there.

One morning a couple of years ago now, Joe was eating breakfast with the kids and he looked outside and shouted, "A cow just ran by our window!"

My first thought was, "What did you put in that coffee?" But sure enough, I looked out and saw a black and white streak in the morning light. We all ran to the windows and the streaks stilled for a moment: Great Danes. Plural. They had gotten loose from a family about three miles down the road and had somehow made their way to our house.

After the cow/dog event I became mildly obsessed with the idea of owning Great Danes. Plural. I wanted two of these gentle giants, and I tossed around names like Kibbles and Bits, Duke and Daisy, Harry and Hermione.

I was convinced it was a sign.

And Joe was, too. But while my sign pointed to *look online for breeders of Great Dane puppies*, Joe's sign had big, bold neon letters that said *NO WAY*.

"You should have seen how many ticks that guy was just picking off that dog! And his entire truck was full of hair."

(He knows, he *knows*, he'll get me with the shedding.)

Our combined objections to getting a dog are pretty typical. Shedding. A yard full of dog poop. The responsibility of racing back to the house to let a dog out (or two), just when we're finally at the point where we have some freedom from diapers and nursing and toddlers and babies, finally at the point where, after ten years, we're able to travel a little.

Oh yeah, and our son is terrified of them.

But oddly, the last reason for not getting a dog also topped the list of why we *should* get a dog. Part of me was convinced that we needed to introduce a dog into Jack's life so he'd become less anxious about them.

Unable to come to a decision, we shelved the idea for a while. But Joey's and Charlie's comments last fall reopened the discussion, for me at least. I decided it was time.

We've always been diligent about making sure Jack does not control our family. It would be easy to let him be bossy and make us eat TV dinners and watch *The Wizard of Oz* nearly every night. But we don't. He eats what we eat and watches what we watch and goes where we go.

Oh sure, our kids will need therapy one day, and they'll sit on the counselor's couch and complain how their mean old mother took away their Wii and how their parents had loud arguments in front of them. But they'll never be able to complain that their brother with special needs held them back.

But hearing Joey and Charlie casually remark to that women in the bleachers that we couldn't get a dog made me realize Jack *was* holding us back. Or, more accurately, the wily snake of anxiety that persists in Jack's mind and soul was holding us back, calling the shots on a family pet.

(Note: Joe was still not completely on board. Oh, he said he'd be happy to get a dog and pay for one of those underground electronic dog fences and listen to the barking and all of that, but he wasn't doing one thing for a pet. Not lifting one finger. He was not coming home from work and putting on anyone's leash or filling a water bowl or using a pooper-scooper. His life, he told me, is demanding enough without picking ticks out of fur or administering heartworm medicine or checking for fleas, thankyouverymuch. In fact, his exact words were, "Carrie, get a dog if you want, but I don't have much more to give." And because I respect my husband, I took this as a signal to proceed full-steam ahead.)

After a lot of deliberation we chose a breed known as a Teddy Bear dog; half-Shih Tzu, half Bichon Frise. Hypoallergenic. No shedding. The polar opposite of the Great Danes I once imagined getting, Teddy Bears only weigh ten or fifteen pounds fully grown, a manageable size for me and, I hoped, Jack.

In February I chose one from a breeder in Maine and put down the deposit, then waited until the puppy would be old enough to come home with us. That would happen in late April, so Joe and I decided to surprise the kids on Easter morning. (Because, as you can imagine, my son who is diagnosed with Autism Spectrum Disorder just *loves* surprises. He loves when we skip over all that social story nonsense and get right to the heart of a stressful situation. Especially if the surprise is a wriggling, squirming ball of fur in the shape of a puppy. In his Easter basket.)

During the time we waited for Easter to come around, I thought a lot about Jack's reaction to a puppy and what I hoped for by bringing one into our family. I hoped the other kids would be thrilled. I hoped the puppy didn't keep me up all night. I hoped there weren't a lot of pee accidents on my new carpet. But ultimately, what I hoped for most was that Jack would decide for himself how he feels about the puppy, instead of anxiety's wily snake hissing into his ear.

I hoped that maybe the best way to tame the serpent was to draw it out into daylight, look straight into its flinty eyes, and hiss right back: *I am the mother and this is my son and you do not decide. You do not decide for me, for Jack, or for our family.*

You do not decide.

Right about now you're probably wondering how it went that Sunday morning. You might be curious to know whether or not Jack packed up his khaki pants and striped shirts and headed out the door, regretting the day he was born into this family, or if introducing a puppy to my autistic, dog-phobic son was a smashing success.

It was not. Through the din of four children laughing and jumping and shouting things like, "I can't believe we have a puppy! Look a puppy!" one robotic voice was unmistakable:

"I did not WANT a DOG. No dog. You have ruined my life."

Joe and I exchanged glances and I looked back at Jack, standing apart from the other kids with his hands clenched to his sides. And I thought to myself, *What have I done?* I don't know why I thought I could conquer this merciless snake so easily.

But later that morning, after the Easter crepes were eaten and we sent the kids upstairs to get dressed for church, Joe stood at the kitchen sink washing the frying pan. He looked over at the puppy's small crate and saw Jack kneeling before it. Quietly, Joe crept over and heard a soft whisper.

"You are. Our first dog. Do not be afraid."

When Joe came upstairs to tell me this, I thought about how life with autism is so very complicated. And as I continue down the rocky path of spectrum disorder alongside my son, I am learning that it is a tender balance of social stories and meltdowns, of risk and reward. Rarely is there smashing success, but some days there are soft whispers of progress.

I thought about how, this time, I just needed to take a leap of faith in him, in me, and in a small puppy we named Wolfie.

Dirty Little Secrets

In a rare display of affection, Jack bounced next to me on our family-room couch where I was sitting with Joe. For a moment we all three sat together, listening to the muted chaos coming from upstairs where the other kids were getting ready for bed.

"At karate," he blurted out unceremoniously, "I keep my autism secret. From my friends."

I turned and looked at his profile while he stared straight ahead.

"Because if they know," he continued in his monotone. "It will be a joke. If they know."

Oh my word, I thought. Does he really think his friends don't know?

I remember holding each baby and asking myself things like, "What will I do when they want to get a tattoo?" or "What will I do if they marry someone I don't like?" But I never once asked myself, "What will I do if my son who has autism wants to keep it a secret from his friends but I've already written a whole book about it?" It just never came up.

Jack himself pointed out how there was an article about our family in the local paper. But some way, somehow, he thinks his friends are still in the dark. Maybe he thinks of autism as his undercover Batman to his public Bruce Wayne, his alter ego, a second self that is separate from his original personality.

What is the right answer here? Was I supposed to lean close to my son and whisper, "Here's the thing, Jack-a-boo. Everyone already knows about your autism. The jig is up."

I think I'd rather tell him there's no Santa Claus.

The process of him finding out he's diagnosed with a spectrum disorder has been painful enough to watch. Every day he asks something new—*Will my autism last forever? Did I catch it like a germ?*—and his once buoyant balloon of self-esteem slowly leaks air with each small discovery.

Of course, there are some good things here that we shouldn't overlook. Jack's theory of mind is expanding to understand that other people have opinions of him; they perceive him. And he wants to be perceived in a certain, non-autistic way. His concern over being a joke amongst his friends is, in fact, progress, even if it is heartbreaking.

He's actually making friends now—something we waited years to see. But the inflexible fabric of his mind has not stretched far enough for him to consider that these friends will—and do—like him for who he is, autism's warts and all.

"But Jack," I protested after a long moment of silence. "There is nothing wrong with having autism. It is nothing to be ashamed of. Your friends like you for who you are."

"No!" he said vehemently, cinching the sash of his dark

blue bathrobe tightly around his waist as he got up to leave. "It will be a joke. If they know."

I guess the obvious question here is: Do I regret revealing Jack to the world before he was ready? And the truth is that I do and I don't.

It's not as if he's been blending in all this time. It's pretty obvious that something is up when we all troop out into public and he jumps and flails and grunts, not to mention the constant chatter about license plates and death. I'm sorry to say it, but there are a million ways in which he looks and acts differently. And, to be honest, some of autism's more visible characteristics—stimming, tantrums, rigidity, sensory processing issues—translate to the world at large as nothing more than bad behavior, overindulgence, disobedience.

So I could let people think Jack was naughty or poorly behaved or weird or annoying, or I could explain he has autism.

I chose to explain autism.

One time in Buffalo I'd taken two-year-old Jack to Walgreens to pick up some pictures. As we waited to pay, he took all the Kit Kat bars from the wire rack in front of the cash register and stacked them up while a woman standing behind us stared at him. He did this every single time we went into that store, and to this day the reason why is still a mystery to me. He didn't want the Kit Kats. He never once tried to open one or taste the chocolate. But he made a beeline for the candy display as soon as we walked in, and with his chubby hands he divided them into large, uneven piles. When it was time to pick them up and leave he would scream and rage, until eventually I scooped him up and walked out the door.

But on this particular trip the woman behind me continued to gape. She was wearing a blue denim jacket and holding a box of white Number 10 envelopes. I wasn't sure what to say, but eventually I turned around and told her, "There is something about this he needs to do. I'm not even sure what it is yet, but he's just been diagnosed with Autism Spectrum Disorder and I think it has to do with that." I watched as her expression relaxed. And as I bent to collect the candy bars from the floor with a red, screaming Jack tucked under one arm, she crouched down to help me with a box of envelopes tucked under hers.

From that point forward I have lived autism right out loud every single day, from Kit Kats to license plates to the kind of toilets that are in the local diner. I have shared what I know and admitted what I don't, I have revealed my own confusion and frustration and inside jokes and tears. Having a son diagnosed with autism has never been one of my dirty little secrets, because keeping this a secret would suggest I am ashamed of it. Of him.

And that would be the cruelest joke of all.

So, no, I don't regret writing about Jack's autism. But I regret that it's unfolding in this particular order: with first the world knowing, and then him.

I regret that I've spent so much time trying to communicate to everyone around me how amazing and fascinating and special autism is, but forgot to communicate the same sentiment to the boy in the blue bathrobe sitting next to me on the couch.

Maybe the answer isn't bursting his private bubble and telling him, "Hey, buddy, your friends all know." Instead, maybe the answer is convincing him to be proud of himself, of his spectrum disorder and his colorful autism. Convincing him that if you give people enough information, if you let them into your life and your world and your beautiful diagnosis, they will hold their envelopes in one hand and help pick up candy bars with the other.

Urgent Caring

"My wrist my wrist my wrist," Jack whimpered, cradling his right arm. He'd just come in from sledding with Rose and Joey on the hill in front of our house where, according to Rose, he'd flipped off the red plastic sled and rolled into the woods.

"Let me see, can you bend it this way?" I asked, moving his fingers back and forth.

"NO!" he screamed. "That hurts, that HURTS!"

"You know what buddy? I think we need to head to urgent care and have this looked at."

"URGENT CARE? What is THAT?"

After a flurry of phone calls, Joe came home early so I could run Jack into the new urgent care center downtown. An hour later my autistic son and I sat waiting in the small exam room to see the doctor on duty. Jack took my phone out of my purse and asked, "Can I text Daddy?"

"Okay, that's fine," I said, reaching for the latest *Woman's World* magazine and relaxing in my chair. All at once I felt very, very tired. For a moment the room was quiet, with him intent on typing and me reading about the latest in crock pot recipes.

"Ugh, Jack, I don't like dinner from the crock pot. Do you? Do you like that chicken thing I make?"

His answer was somewhat unrelated to my question, which is not unusual. "I texted Daddy. I tolded him we should go to Shorty's tonight. For dinner."

"You *told* him, Jack. Right? 'Tolded' isn't a word, you *told* him."

"Yes. I tolded him."

Before I could take my grammar lesson any further, the doctor knocked quickly on the exam room door and hurried inside, not waiting for an answer.

"Okay, okay now," she said brightly, scanning the computer screen on the table. "Jack! How are you? I just have a few questions. Let's see . . . do you have any allergies?"

"No, he—" I started to answer, but he cut me off.

"YES! I am allergic to CITRUS FRUIT."

"What? No you aren't! Really, he isn't. He has no allergies." I stared at him with my best you-better-stop-this-crap-right-now face. It didn't work.

He looked over at me as if we'd never met before—as if I had not delivered all nine pounds, three ounces of him out of my own body and nursed him for seven months and taught him how to sign *mama* with his chubby little fingers. "I DO! I am allergic. To me they are sour. So I am allergic."

"Well," I cleared my throat and narrowed my eyes back at him. "The citrus allergy, is, um, unconfirmed at this point."

"Ah, okay," she said, turning to where he sat on the exam table. "Jack, where does your wrist hurt?"

"How did Jesus know he was going to DIE at the LAST SUPPER?"

The doctor looked up in surprise and shot me a quick look.

"He's kind of been interested in that sort of thing. You know, lately," I said. She looked back at me blankly.

"He has A-U-T-I-S-M-F-Y-I," I blurted out, like a contestant in some bizarre spelling bee. I'm never certain exactly when or how I should assert the whole diagnosis thing. I mean, he's nine now, and kids who are nine don't usually ask about the Last Supper or Jesus or pretend they're allergic to limes.

Sometimes I try to pre-empt the matter a little. Whenever I call to make an appointment for him, I explain he has autism and it may make communication a little tricky. But you can't exactly do that with a place like urgent care.

One time I took him to our regular doctor and as the nurse led us back to an exam room, I noticed the word AUTISM written in large, bold letters across his chart. They must have used a black permanent Sharpie marker, the kind Jack once used to write all over the walls in our Buffalo home—just a week before we put the house up for sale.

If you had asked me about how I felt seeing AUTISM written on his chart that way, I would have told you I absolutely didn't mind. In fact, I was grateful the office thought to clue everyone in so Jack's visit could be as successful as possible.

But I'd have to admit that it did nag at me for a while afterwards, and I couldn't put my finger on exactly why. Was it the size of the letters? Or was it my own insecurity, my deep, unacknowledged shame about having a special-needs son?

In urgent care, the doctor finished up the exam quickly, and in between answering questions about Moses and what kind of toilet she prefers—Kohler or American Standard—determined Jack had nothing more than a sprained wrist. At last, to my great relief, she left the room.

"Jack!" I hissed. "What's with the toilets! You know we said no more asking people about their toilets."

"What," he said smugly. "It's good information to know."

"And give me my phone back. What are you texting Daddy about?"

"I tolded you! I want to go to Shorty's."

"It's *told*. You *told* me, Jack."

As we walked out of the urgent care with a hearty goodbye and Jack whisper-shouting, "That doctor SMELLED FUNNY!" I thought again about the word AUTISM written in black and white.

One of the first essays I ever wrote about Jack was called "Paper Boy," about my intent to bring him to life beyond his paper diagnosis; an attempt to add dimension to the flatness of the clinical phrase *Autism Spectrum Disorder*.

But sometimes I wonder how much of Jack's progress depends on what I choose to see on any given day: It's a good day if he wears his eye patch without a scene, a bad day if he's stimming a lot. Good if he does his homework without much drama, bad if he asks me ninety million times where I first saw the movie *Annie*.

Good bad good good bad good bad bad. It's exhausting.

This is my life with Jack. It is living with the undulating

rhythm of lost dreams and new hopes. It's *oh wow he doesn't really ask about death anymore! But now he's obsessing about the Keurig and every time I look at the Keurig he's standing over it and trying to take it apart and counting the K-cups and rearranging them in some mysterious order and I am going to go straight out of my mind.*

Driving home in the dark, it occurred to me that I can bring him off of the paper, but I sometimes forget to add the color; the wild splashes of yellow laughter and the brilliant red tantrums and the pale pink butterfly kisses and the long silvery threads of anxiety weaving in and around his soul.

Autism is bigger than a black marker on a white piece of paper; it is musings about Catholicism and plans for family dinner and sore (but not fractured) wrists. It's pretending to be allergic to lemons and stimming in urgent care and a robotic voice that *tolded* me he wanted to go out for dinner as a family.

And my reaction to the block letters was—like autism itself—complicated, a combination of sadness and gratitude and surprise and bewilderment.

Later that night we all sat crowded in a booth at Shorty's. I looked down the bench seat to where Jack sat, squished between five-year-old Henry and ten-year-old Joey. He was grabbing tortilla chips from the basket in front of him, rocking slightly and grunting to himself.

I resisted the urge to put a hand on his shoulder to try and still him, or to ask him if we should head to the lobby so he could get his zoomies out. I didn't chide him for eating too fast. Instead, I focused on his small smile, the way he pushed his glasses up the bridge of his nose, his obvious pleasure at being together.

In the restaurant, I chose to see J-A-C-K, instead of just A-U-T-I-S-M. I saw the rainbow of moods and emotions and potential that is my son, and for the briefest moment, I savored the wholeness of him. For the moment, it was just *good*.

Next time I call for an appointment, I thought to myself, I'll tell them that yes he has autism and yes it may make communication a little tricky. But I'll also tell them they won't even believe how funny he is.

I'll add some color to autism's black and white canvas.

Puppy Remorse

A *lot* of people warned me that I would experience buyer's remorse the first few weeks after Wolfie came home. They cautioned that I might regret adopting a puppy: the mess, the barking, the tiny puddles on the floor.

I am happy to report that I do not regret having Wolfie, not one little bit. What I do regret is having kids. And a husband.

With five kids, our household is fairly chaotic. Loud. Add a puppy (one who resembles a living stuffed animal) to the mix and, well, their heads just about exploded from the excitement of it all. I worried Wolfie's hair might start to fall out from all the petting.

During his entire first week home my children raced downstairs at 5:30 in the morning. For what, you so rightly ask? What could be happening in my kitchen at 5:30 a.m. that desperately needed the attention of five kids?

Why, a puppy, of course! A puppy asleep in his crate, quite comfortably, thankyouverymuch, but whom apparently *must* be woken up. And every single time I sit down to work or start making dinner or attempt to talk on the phone,

one of them rushes in to exclaim that the puppy sneezed/snorted/moved/whined/existed.

"Mom! Look! He's drinking his water!"

"Mom! Come quick! He stopped drinking his water!"

"Oh! Now he's having more! MORE WATER!"

Wolfie's like some fascinating toy and they just can't stop reporting on his behavior. It has made them move even faster and shout even louder. (Especially five-year-old Henry, who was loud enough to begin with.)

I, on the other hand, want to slow everything down. I want to do exactly what I didn't do when I had newborns. I want to let the laundry pile up and step over the vacuum and order take-out so I can have more time to gaze into the puppy's beautiful brown eyes. I want to squeal about how *cu-ute* his little nugget poops are, and giggle when he nips at my toes. I want to shrug my shoulders and smile tiredly at the sleep deprivation because, really, it's all worth it.

Except it's not worth it because it's not the puppy who deprives me of sleep; it's the five people I thought I had already sleep-trained and taught to stay in their beds all night. The ones I had made repeat back to me *a tired mama is a mean mama* as extra motivation.

But Wolfie and I? We are simpatico. We love each other. He doesn't look at me with a five-year-old's belligerence or a tween's disgust. He doesn't ask annoying questions about the credit card bill or say the toothpaste is *too spicy* or beg for waffles when I've already made pancakes.

I came up with sweet nicknames: Wolfers, Wolfman, the big W. Pup-pup and Pupperdoodle.

Joe asked what he could do to get me to love him as

much as I do the puppy. I told him, "Easy. Gaze at me adoringly all day and then go sleep in a crate all night."

All week I took control of everything related to Wolfie. I wrote up a schedule for crate training and I shouted mean things like, "Who will clean up his mess if he has an accident? I WILL! So we're going to do it MY WAY!"

I insisted only I could hold the leash because he really likes to walk down the driveway with *me*, and whenever one of them tried to lead him I snapped, "You don't know how to make him walk! He's just wandering around!"

I barked—pun intended—at all of them to leave the poor dog alone for five minutes, while at the same time trying to cajole Jack into petting him, holding him, walking him.

By the middle of the week I was an exhausted shell of a person. My eyes felt grainy and my head weighed about a hundred pounds. To break up the afternoon and give the poor animal a chance to rest, I decided we should take a trip to HomeGoods to pick out a new dog bed.

Right away I found the perfect one. It was chic. It was retro. It matched perfectly the warm gold walls in our family room. And even better, it had a soft, fluffy cushion for little Wolfman to lay his sweet head.

Jack, apparently, also thought he'd found the perfect one. "No. Mom. No. This one. It's better," he told me, holding up a tan bed shaped like a dog house.

"Oh, Jack. That one is okay, but I think he'll like this one better."

On and on we bickered in the middle of the store, while Henry crawled around pretending, "I Wolfie! I like a puppy!" and Rose tried to put a collar on him. I clutched my bed even closer to my chest and thought, "What do you care? You don't even like him!"

This isn't exactly true, if I'm being honest. There have been baby steps between Jack and Wolfie, between autism and puppy. Over the course of the week Jack has started engaging with Wolfie in his own way: by taking control. He organizes all of the logistics related to his water and food, leash and toy placement. It's usually the first step in any of Jack's meaningful relationships; he likes to be in charge.

Unfortunately, so do I.

"But this one is so much better," I wheedled.

"This is good. It's a DOG HOUSE. He will love it." Jack insisted.

"Fine!" I sneered spitefully, wondering briefly why Fake Mom refused to make an appearance. "Let's buy both and let Wolfie decide!" So out of HomeGoods we trotted, my bed under my arm, Jack's plush doghouse under his. As soon as we got home he set them up in the puppy's play area, side by side.

Friday morning wasn't much better. I snapped at all the kids for wanting to hold the leash as we walked down the driveway, and Rose boarded the bus with tears in her eyes. Driving Joey to school, I sighed a long sigh and told him I was sorry, it had been a rough week. I confessed I wasn't really sure what I was doing.

He took a big bite of his egg and cheese wrap, nodded, and agreed.

"You know what, Mom? A character in the book I'm reading said, 'Don't just steer. Drive.' Maybe you're trying to, you know, steer too much."

I looked over at him. "Boochie," I said, using the nickname we've called him since he was a tiny baby. "I think maybe you're right."

After I kissed him goodbye and dropped him off at school, I thought about steering as opposed to driving, *controlling* versus *keeping in motion*.

I remembered how I did, in fact, hold him when he was a newborn; how I stepped over the vacuum and called Joe at work to bring home Thai food so I wouldn't have to cook. How I traced the whorls on the inside of his ears and stroked his thick dark hair.

Pulling into Crossfit, I vowed to stop steering, to stop trying to control everything. To let go and lengthen the leash and wander around without a destination. In fact, I decided to let our tiny puppy drive for a little while. I have a feeling he'll take us where we need to go.

As for the dog bed Wolfie chose? Well, he circled both beds once, twice, and then hopped into the light tan doghouse, while Jack stood outside of the play area, watching intently.

I held my breath for a moment, and heard Jack murmur so quietly I almost didn't catch it, "I knowded he'd want that one. I just did."

A View from the Floor

Allow me to introduce myself. My name is Wolfie. I am half Bichon and half Shih-Tzu, also known as a Teddy Bear dog or a Zuchon (or sometimes a Shichon). I am sixteen-and-a-half pounds and I barely stand a foot off the floor, but do not let my size fool you. I may be small, but I am mighty.

I've been with my family for five months now. Everyone keeps saying the Easter Bunny brought me as a surprise. But I remember the two biggest people in the family—the mom and the dad people—came to pick me up in a conference center off the highway in a small town called Portsmouth. We drove around for hours and then snuck home because they said the kids were finally asleep. I never did see a bunny.

It's important to fit in with a new family right away, so for the first two weeks I was in my new home, I tried this strategy:

Pee on couch. Look adorable.

Poop on rug. Appear irresistible.

Pee on floor. Tilt head to one side with cutest expression possible.

This went on for a while until the dad guy said I was on something called *thin ice* and I'd better get house-trained soon. He had just stepped in one of my puddles wearing only his socks.

He pretends he doesn't like me, this dad. But I'm not fooled by him. When it's late at night and all the small people have gone to bed and the mom is upstairs reading, he sits on the big red couch and he calls to me in a quiet voice.

"Wolf, come on boy, come sit with me."

I sit next to him and we watch shows that the mom doesn't like: baseball and politics and something weird called *The First 48*. But I can tell by the absent-minded way he rubs my foot that he's only half-listening to the television. Instead he's thinking about words in his head, words like *patients* and *children* and *tax returns* and *healthcare* and *insurance*.

There are a lot of people in this house. Seven. Two big people and five small ones, ones the big people call *kiddos*. One time a man came and delivered some food in a brown paper bag that smelled delicious. When he stepped into the kitchen and saw all the *kiddos* at the counter, he asked if we were having a birthday party.

The round boy laughed and shouted, "Yes! It my birthday! Let's sing HAPPY BIRTHDAY TO ME! Happy birthday to me!" until the mom said, "Okay, Henry, we heard you. Eat your egg roll."

This Henry kiddo is the smallest, but he isn't too small. Life is very, very exciting for him, and he is very loud about it all. He fills up every room with his chatter and his laughter and his drawings, and he is squishy and delicious and curious and smart. He is so alive, you can almost see his heart beating through his favorite Batman shirt.

There are all these boys and only one little girl. When you look at her you just think about the color pink. She is sweetness and light and airy and calm, like the most delicate wafer cookie you hold on your tongue until it melts.

She works very hard. She is the first one awake to take me out in the morning, even before I ask, and all day long she is trying to do things for other people, packing their snacks or sweeping the floor or straightening the playroom.

Her mother worries and the Dad guy hopes if he tells her how beautiful and smart and sweet she is, she will believe it forever and never listen if someone accuses her of being fat or ugly or stupid or worthless. I'm not worried, though, because this pink girl is so very strong.

There is a very big boy, a boy who stands taller than the mom's shoulder. He wears glasses. They call him a *tween* sometimes, and I don't know what that means but it seems to annoy him. It must be some kind of *kiddo*. He and the mom can really get each other laughing. They both like the same jokes. But there is a strain that I don't think was there before. It feels new. It feels like the beginning of something and the end of something all at the same time. He is starting to cleave from them, to long for video games and something called an *iPhone* and for movies that are *PG-13*. The mom, she knows this, and her heart is aching to make the most of the time she has left, before this *tween* will pack up his glasses and his gym shorts and his Nook and drive down the driveway to a faraway place called *college*.

I may be very close to the floor, but I see it all.

There's another big boy, just about as tall as the first boy. He also wears glasses. From behind they look like the same boy and sometimes people mix them up, but I never do.

From what I understand, I was supposed to help this boy. He has something called *autism* and he was very, very afraid of dogs, even little ones like me.

When the mom first brought me in from the garage where I was hiding and trying to stay very, very quiet, all of the other kids squealed and laughed and clapped their hands. But he didn't. His face was all twisted up and his voice was very loud and angry sounding.

"I DO NOT like dogs. You have ruined my life. With this dog."

I don't know anything about *autism* or how to help people who have it. So I just did the only thing I knew how: I waited. I waited and waited and one afternoon when no one was watching he crept over to where I was lying on the couch. With one finger he stroked my paw.

"You are. Soft."

Sometimes this boy gets very, very mad. One day his temper rose until it felt like the sun was shining inside the house, the rays too hot to touch. He was screaming and hitting his head over and over again.

"No para! I will not have a PARA!"

I did not know what a *para* was, but the mom seemed to because she kept talking softly, telling him to take a deep breath and calm down, they would talk about it.

Then he came for her. With his fists curled into the tightest balls he charged her wordlessly. She grabbed his wrists and held them with her long fingers and said, "Enough

Jack," so sharply her voice was like a knife cutting through the hot, still room. He dropped his arms to his sides and the only sound was his whimpering, *no para no para no para*.

I barked once, twice, my voice not as sharp as hers, more like an ice cube clattering into a smooth glass. He fell to his knees next to me and buried his fingers into the fur around my neck, where it's longest and deepest. Through his fingertips, I understood. I knew. Somehow, because of this strange thing called a *para*, the boy felt different. He felt worried and alone and disappointed.

He felt *less*.

There is another boy. He looks just like the dad, with dark hair and deep brown eyes that make you think of chocolate. He is all fun, this one.

But every once in a while a shadow crosses his face and his eyes get cloudy, like the rain is coming. That's when I know he needs a little extra cuddle and I just turn on my back so he can rub my soft, white belly. He rubs it until the sun shines again.

"Come on, Wolfie, run outside with me!"

Not long ago this big yellow bus started coming around. We all walked down to the bus stop and everyone was so excited. But when the *kiddos* got on and the bus pulled away, the mom put her head on the dad guy's shoulder and said, "Oh, Joe."

Slowly the three of us walked back up the driveway. They looked down and started talking to me in a funny voice with funny words. "You a wittle doggy, wight? Just a wittle pup-pup." I felt confused at first, but then I understood. Their babies were gone. Now I was the baby.

Last weekend we all went to a big field to play with a black and white ball. The mom and dad kicked it around with the *kiddos*, but the second boy said he only wanted to hold my leash and run with me.

So we did. We ran and ran through the fields together. And with each big step he took I could tell that, for the moment, he was free. Free of the shame and rage and confusion and panic that follow him around all day like uninvited guests.

Running by my side through the rich green grass, he wasn't a child with *autism* or a fifth grader with a *para* or a brother who is not like the rest.

He was, quite simply, just a boy and his dog.

Mirror, Mirror on the Wall

I took Jack for a follow-up appointment to the pediatric ophthalmologist last week.

I wish I could tell you it went well. To be honest, I expected it to go well. Ever since the teachers at school wore their glasses and convinced Jack that eyewear was no big deal, he's been diligent about wearing his electric-blue specs every single day.

So when the time came for the follow-up, I thought, "It'll be fine. We're done with all that drama."

Yeah. No.

The night before the appointment he started to ramp up, declaring in a bossy tone that he was not going to any dumb eye doctor. Because his eyes were better! He could see! The next morning—after failed attempts at trickery that included doughnuts, a new playlist, and total control over the radio on the drive—I finally had to haul him into the car, kicking and screaming.

He cried off and on the whole way there. For an hour and eighteen minutes.

Then he refused to get out of the car. There were more

attempts at trickery, more offers of lunch in Boston and Taylor Swift downloads and new art supplies, and finally, more hauling. Once inside, he sneered at the receptionist, "I do not need to be here. I can SEE!" She nodded sympathetically.

After we'd sat in the waiting room for a while with Jack kicking the leg of my chair even though I told him a million times to stop it, an adorable little boy named Alec stumbled in with his eyes dilated and started to shout things like *it's very dark in here* really loudly because he also had hearing aids and Jack said *stop yelling we can hear you*. Finally we were called in for his exam.

The doctor was very pleased with Jack's progress. So pleased, in fact, that she suggested we start patching his strong eye right away, and prescribed two hours a day for the next four months.

Jack, who rarely listens in on a conversation that doesn't directly pertain to when toothpaste was invented or what time Cinemagic opens, looked up from the black plastic eye shield he was fiddling with and said quietly, "No patch. I am not wearing a patch."

The doctor and I exchanged knowing smiles. To be more accurate, hers was knowing. Mine was more like *I don't know how I'm going to get him to do this.* I stuffed the pile of patches into my purse.

On our way home I suggested we stop at Target and buy a movie to watch that evening with his patch on. My spirits buoyed just so slightly when he grumbled, "Fine. *Oz the Great and Powerful*. I want that movie." Great, I thought to myself. He'll settle down and watch it and it will be fine. Crisis averted and I am the most awesome mom ever!

Yeah. No.

As soon as we walked in the door and I paid the babysitter, I announced brightly that we'd bought a new movie. And we were going to watch it! Right now! Excitement! Popcorn! Much bustling about for special cozy blankets and pillow pets!

Except for Jack.

"I'm not wearing that FREAKING PATCH!" he screamed and twirled like a tornado wearing an orange striped shirt, clutching *Oz the Great and Powerful* so hard his knuckles were white.

I pried the movie out of his hands and passed it to Joey like a track star in a relay race, telling him to get it started in hopes it would calm his frantic brother. Then I grabbed a patch, tore off the paper, and managed to seal it around Jack's right eye. I thought if he could just feel it, try it, understand that it doesn't hurt, he'd settle down.

Yeah. No.

Jack is not aggressive by nature; his instincts are not to lash out and hurt. But the fact of the matter is, as he gets older his anger is intensifying, strengthening, escalating. And managing the whirlwind that is my nearly eighty-pound son, with all his flailing arms and legs, is becoming something of a challenge.

Even worse is the effect his tantrums have on the other people in our house. I glanced over at the couch where the rest of the kids were seated, patiently waiting for James

Franco to begin his journey to Oz. "Mom," Charlie said shakily. "Just let him take it off. Please."

"Jack," I said, struggling to keep my voice even. "You are upsetting everyone. You need to stay in your room until you feel more in control."

I followed close behind as he stomped up the stairs, shrieking and sobbing, and watched as he threw himself on his bed and thrust his head under the pillow. I could barely make out his muffled words, but I heard part of his chant, and it sounded something like, *look weird I look weird people will say I am weird.*

And so, inside the storm there is continued progress. A subtle—yet monumental—shift in perspective continues inside Jack's rigid brain. Jack is slowly realizing that other people see him, that they have opinions different than his own. He is becoming aware of himself.

Leaning against the doorway of his room, watching as he shook his head over and over and over underneath his pillow, I considered what this shift really means. It means he is starting more and more to *flex*. He's beginning to understand *there is you* and *you see me*. And in the eyes of others he is glimpsing a mirrored reflection, one that says *you are weird* and *you are not normal.*

Part Three: Bajillions

Ever since Jack was a toddler, our goal has been to make sure he fits into the world as best he can while always respecting the limits of his autism.

This was unconscious on our part in a lot of ways, but I believe it was always in the back of our minds, jangling around like the loose change you find underneath the cushions on the couch. We knew he needed to learn manners, and to say *please* and *thank you* just like everyone else. He had to eat what we ate and sleep when we slept and go to church with his family.

In short, he could not get special treatment simply because of his diagnosis.

And yet there are times when we need to flex and bend for him, to soften the edges and dim the lights when his world becomes too loud, too bright, too crunchy, too much. Thus emerged the everlasting balancing act, what it means to live with a spectrum disorder.

At the beginning of every school year Joe and I talk

about whether or not Jack's in the right place. Should we move him out of public school and into a setting filled with others like him, where he can learn math at his own pace and stim in wide, open spaces? Or do we keep him moving forward—stumbling forward, in some cases—to the beat of a drum that doesn't come close to matching his rhythm, in hopes that he'll eventually pick up some of its tempo and learn to dance along?

It's as though we're trying to fit the pieces of a puzzle together, but one piece is not like the others, does not want to fit in exactly. Its edges are different: round where the rest are square and rigid where many are flexible. Some days I feel like we keep pushing and pushing this one piece into place but it simply will not go. It will not fit.

Then Jack will do something to surprise us—he'll make a joke or triumph over anxiety's cruel snake long enough to stroke Wolfie's soft ear. He'll taste the lasagna he doesn't usually like and he'll wear the glasses he doesn't really want to wear.

And then Joe and I will agree: he's exactly where he should be.

A big piece of the puzzle is Jack's own discovery of his autism. Now he is struggling to understand where he fits into our family, his school, and the world. He longs to know others like him.

His reaction to his diagnosis has been unwavering; he does not like to be different or unlike others—he *does not want this autism in me*. As his mother I can't imagine what this must feel like, this rejection of one's self, of something that is so intrinsically his.

I've always loved this quote by Albert Einstein:

"If you judge a fish by its ability to climb a tree, you'll spend your whole life believing it's stupid."

Whenever I see this, I think *let him be a fish*. Not a tree-climbing, bark-gripping fish, but a shimmery silver fish, sleek and weightless in crystal blue water.

Let him glide through our pond at home and into the wide world beyond.

And as he paddles and floats and kicks through the clear water, I hope he stops for a moment to notice how unique everyone around him really is; all of the colors and shapes and sizes in his ocean, from rigid coral to smooth, slippery eels, powerful great white sharks and quiet turtles.

Hopefully Jack will one day figure out that with all that is different around him, he will most certainly find a place to fit.

May Jack be a fish, and continue doing all the things he's good at, like being a superhero brother and spelling tricky words and sailing down our long driveway on his silver scooter. And swimming.

Swim, Jack. Swim like a fish.

May you feel the cool rush of water on your face, your body light and buoyant as you sail through the streams of fifth grade and summer school and *why do I have an aide and no one else does*. Swim, and the rest will follow.

Because fish don't know how to climb trees. They also don't know how to do algebra or spelling sentences, or how to pray in church. Their sleek bodies aren't built for soccer or running or hiking; they're built for swimming, for navigating vast oceans and clear lakes. Their minds aren't wired to read people's expressions or understand geometry or figure out how important it is to be polite.

Fish do what they're good at; they swim together and hunt for food and swim again. They never stop moving. And fish survive. They thrive, flourish even. In fact, they even find schools of other fish just like them.

And you know what else I think fish do? When the water is quiet and calm and smooth and no one is watching, I think fish dance.

Autism Smart

"Can you believe Jack made this?" the karate instructor said, handing me a small white flag.

"He did?" I asked, turning the piece of fabric over in my hands. It was roughly the size of an index card.

"Yes!" she said excitedly. "All on his own. We told them to use the space to describe themselves, and that's what he drew."

He'd colored boxes in the four corners of the rectangle. In the center were four hearts. His handwriting slanted uphill just the tiniest bit, but the boxes were drawn with ruler-precision, one word in each one.

Care.

Love.

Nice.

Autism.

And in the center with those four hearts were the words *the hearts of awareness* written unevenly in red marker.

Hearts of awareness.

I looked back at her face, open and sweet, and noted her eyes had a glimmer of tears.

"I just think it's so amazing, what he wrote."

"Oh, it is! Amazing."

But standing in the lobby of the karate studio, picking all five kids up from camp, I felt almost disconnected from Jack's artwork. For some reason I didn't feel thrilled or excited or emotional in the least. I felt nothing.

Just then all five kids rushed up the stairs to where I stood, Jack sandwiched between two of his brothers.

"Hey! Jack! Did you—"

"Do NOT ASK ME about that FLAG!"

"Okay Jack, calm down. Let's go."

And home we went, to an afternoon of badminton and swimming. But I kept thinking about the flag, and whenever I caught a glimpse of it on the counter, jumbled amongst the rest of the papers and artwork from camp that day, I felt uneasy.

I asked Jack about it a few times during the day.

"Nothing. I don't know."

"What do you mean you don't know?"

"I don't know why I wrote it. It is just done."

Later that night, as I was cleaning the kitchen after dinner and putting the day's paperwork away, I realized why the flag bothered me: it didn't seem like something he was, well, smart enough to think of and draw.

A lot of times people comment on how smart Jack is; how uncannily brilliant people on the spectrum tend to be.

Huh, I usually say to myself. *You think?*

I'm not saying this to be mean. Joe and I have five kids and, without naming names, we have one who is quite bright but incorrigibly lazy, two hard workers and one bound for juvie, the last, obviously, being five-year-old Henry. As with any group, we have what I would consider a range of intelligence.

And then we have Jack. Jack's brain is about as easy to deconstruct as hieroglyphics written inside a pyramid. It's tricky. Yes, he has an extensive memory for seemingly random information: when we last went to Dairy Queen, what time *Caillou* is on, how old Rosa Parks was when she died. But does this ceaseless acquisition of obscure information mean a person is smart? Is the constant cataloging of dates and times and Oreo Blizzards a sign of intelligence?

Merriam-Webster defines *smart* as "very good at learning or thinking about things, and showing intelligence or good judgment."

You see? This definition doesn't mention one single thing about Disney movies or memorizing license plates or what color Monday might be. And we all know about his occasional lack of judgment, especially when it comes to things like conversations about toilets.

How, exactly, does he process information? Is he Merriam-Webster-smart about it?

He *is* good at a lot of things. He now makes breakfast independently (well, mostly) and he's figured out how to manipulate the Rubik's Cube so two sides have solid colors. And he always, always reminds me when my nephew's birthday is.

But there are other things that remain out of his grasp. Consistent with a spectrum diagnosis, Jack has a difficult time understanding our moods and expressions. He is always astonished when I get aggravated over things like his asking me ninety-thousand times if I've yet bought the tickets to see *Maleficent*.

At age ten, he is painfully naïve. He believes every single car commercial he sees, and thought Breast Cancer Awareness month meant women only get breast cancer during October. (He pronounced it *breest* cancer, by the way.) And socially? Well, please. Social cues are like another language for our Jack. I mean, why wouldn't you tell one of the teachers at school to stop wearing that purple plaid skirt she wears because it's so ugly it makes you *sick*?

Just before he went to bed I asked him one more time about the flag, what made him think to write *hearts of awareness* and to color a heart blue.

"Because. They are always saying LIGHT IT UP BLUE for autism." I nodded, still feeling a little unconvinced.

"Go now. I don't want to talk about that FLAG anymore.

The next morning the kids all had karate camp again, but five-year-old Henry was difficult to rouse. He stayed nestled in bed long after the other four were downstairs eating breakfast, only his chubby round face showing above his blankets.

We each took turns calling up to him, and I grew irritated while I organized the other kids' lunches and bathing suits.

"Henry! You are making us late and you are going to miss breakfast!"

Eventually he wandered downstairs, wearing a red striped shirt and mismatching shorts. "I was sleepin'," he announced proudly.

"Henry, LOOK!" Jack shouted. We all turned and saw him

standing at the toaster, buttering a warm bagel. "I made you BREAKFAST. So you can EAT. We won't be LATE."

I paused for a second. "Uh, Jack?"

"WHAT? No talking now, we will be late."

So I turned back to the whirlwind of our morning routine, packing bags and applying sunscreen and shuttling them all out the door. But once I dropped them off and waved goodbye, I came back to the quiet house and noticed the flag sitting on my desk. I turned it over in my hand again.

Care.

Love.

Nice.

Autism.

Hearts of awareness.

I thought about how Jack worried about me all October long, counseling me in his monotone voice about mammograms and telling us to wear pink for "Breest" Cancer Awareness.

I thought about his progress with Wolfie over the past few months, his slow and steady steps moving from *you have ruined my life* to furtive pets and eventual walks. Now, together, they run.

I thought about *awareness*, that feeling of noticing that something exists.

I thought about breest cancer and bagels and hearts filled in with brightly colored markers.

I decided there is Merriam-Webster smart. And then there is autism smart.

Autism smart is learning the things that come so easily

for everyone else, things like caring and loving and being nice enough to toast a bagel so your brother doesn't go to camp hungry.

It is pushing past the heartbreak of *I am different* to dream of the bright blue lights beyond. It is conquering a phobia and racing a small tan puppy around the yard.

Sure, Jack has more to learn than most. He has to learn to stop asking strangers how much they weigh and how old they are, and to maybe ask only three times instead of forty what time the movie starts. He needs to recognize a smile. But this doesn't mean he's not smart. It just means his mountain is a little higher, a little steeper, a little harder to climb. But climb it he will.

Going to Church

I'm sorry to say this, but I don't like going to church. Mostly I don't like going because church makes my family look bad, bringing out the worst in us. It exposes us as the loud, messy group we are; it puts all of us on display for the congregation to judge.

I rarely go. Instead, on Sunday mornings I opt for the hot room of Bikram yoga, ninety minutes of meditative exercise and quiet reflection.

Joe usually takes all five kids to church on his own, and I suspect he secretly leaves his wedding ring at home so he can capitalize on all those sympathetic smiles he gathers like dollar bills in the collection basket. ("Poor man!" at least a few people must think. "All alone with five children!") But during our previous evening's Saturday night date—a promise we made years ago to each other and have practically never missed—he asked if, since it was Lent and all, I could skip yoga just this once and go to Mass with him. He mentioned how the kids ask for me every week; he claimed church just doesn't feel complete without our entire family.

Foolishly (and possibly influenced by the French Martini

I was drinking at the time) I agreed. And so that next morning seven Cariellos went to 10:30 Mass.

We pulled into the crowded parking lot about three minutes before the start of Mass and hurried through the double glass doors and down the side aisle. Jack was at the head of our line and he insisted on choosing where we sat. Every ten rows or so he would stop, survey the long wooden bench, and loudly declare, "NO! NOT THIS ONE!" while six Cariello's piled up behind him. Finally, at approximately 10:31, he picked seats way up front, about three rows from the altar.

Once we sat down, I looked over and saw the hem of Charlie's favorite football jersey hanging below the sweater he'd hastily thrown on because I'd asked him *one hundred million times* to change into something a little more appropriate than a shirt with a Patriots logo and Tom Brady's name across the back. I also noticed that somehow, in the shuffle to leave the house, Rose's hair hadn't been brushed; her fine blond locks were tangled around her head like a knotted halo.

Something about the light in church forces me to notice every wrinkled shirt, every creased collar, every butter stain on my kids' clothes. Even worse, the sunlight slanting through the stained glass seems to beam directly into each of their ear canals, exposing weeks—maybe months—of ear wax built up. It's hard to feel particularly spiritual under such circumstances.

You can kind of tell the people who don't go to church that often because, well, they sort of changed a bunch of things and the infrequent attenders notice it. And by "infrequent attenders," I mean me. Joe smirked over in my direction as I struggled to keep up with the new verses.

(Note: This is a good time to introduce the concept of irony: a man who lures his wife to church under the pretense of religious commitment, but then spends most of the hour making fun of her.)

As luck would have it, I drew the short straw and wound up sitting squashed between Henry and Jack, perhaps the two worst churchgoers in all of Catholicism. Four-year-old Henry is probably the loudest person I've ever known, and Jack, well, I probably don't need to go into a whole lot of explanation about why Mass is difficult for Jack. The clanging bells, the need to remain still, the idea that the Communion Host represents someone's actual body. None of this goes over well with a boy who has a tendency to take everything literally.

As Jack rifled through my purse, Henry belted out "Where the man who naked? Why he covered up?" I glared at Joe, asking *What kind of church do you take them to every week?* with my eyes, and he gestured to the statue of Jesus, covered in deep purple velvet for the Lenten season.

Just then, Jack held up a ChapStick and shouted, "Why do you have THIS?" before applying it liberally to his lips, his eyelids, and his ear lobes. "Do I smell like a CHERRY?" I longed for my yoga mat, for the deep hush of the hot room, for the freedom to stretch and bend.

Then, in between the first and second reading, the best thing possible happened: Henry fell asleep. In the warm church he curled up on my lap, started to suck his thumb, and closed his blue eyes.

In the quiet space between Jack's stimming and rocking and yelling out page numbers in the song book, I thought back to a time when Joe and I went to church in Buffalo, when we were a young married couple without children. A few pews ahead of us had sat a father and his teenage son. The boy had wild, curly dark hair sticking straight out from his head, and wore a dirty ski coat and a sullen expression. He looked surly and greasy. I remember vowing I would never let my son walk out of the house like that, how I would have made that boy take a shower and slick down his unruly hair, would have forced him to put on something other than a stained jacket.

But when the time came for the sign of peace, where parishioners offer each other a handshake, that father turned towards his gangly son, heartily embraced him with both arms, and exuberantly told him, "I love you."

I've thought of that moment every now and again over the years, and sitting in church with my own disheveled children I realized this memory has stayed with me for a reason. Church is not a place for judgment or shame, but a place of acceptance and belonging. A place where you watch your children grow through the years of sweet cherry ChapStick and knotted hair and dirty jackets. That, indeed, families are messy, but our love for one another endures things like ear wax and autism, stimming and *what song are we on now*.

When it came time for communion I stayed seated, holding Henry's sleepy warm body on my lap as Joe and the other kids filed by me to the center aisle. As each of the four children passed us by, they stopped for a moment to pat Henry's head and smile while he dozed and dreamed. Rose gestured to the family behind us and whispered, "This is my baby brother," as she caressed his fuzzy brown crew cut.

Letters from a Secret Admirer

Last Tuesday I headed out to meet the bus at 2:40 p.m., stopping to collect the mail at the bottom of our driveway. As I stood organizing the sheaf of brightly colored flyers and bills into a manageable pile, a light blue Honda Odyssey slowed to a stop and the driver opened her window. A pretty blonde woman poked her head out and said tentatively, "Carrie?"

It was my neighbor from around the corner. I'd spoken with her a handful of times: once while I was handing out Halloween candy on our darkened front porch, a few times at the school's noisy open house. I know her well enough to nod and wave, but sometimes I have trouble retrieving her name right away. Carol—no, not Carol. Catherine? Uh-uh. Cynthia! Ah yes, Cynthia, with four small children scattered in and around the same grades as my own kids. She passes me every day while I wait for the bus, and we always exchange a smile.

"Hello!" I said heartily, still mentally scanning my memory for her husband's name. "How are you?"

We exchanged pleasantries for a moment or so, and I

noticed she seemed a little nervous, excited. She explained how she sees Jack a lot in school and heard about his fascination with license plates, and she turned to pick something up out of the passenger side and passed it through the window. An Illinois license plate.

"I wasn't sure, I didn't know when to give it to him. But I wanted him to have it." I could see in her cautious smile this gesture meant nearly as much to her as it did to me. My eyes filled and I stuck the upper half of my body through her car window to embrace her. "Thank you," I told her again and again. "Thank you for thinking of him."

This was not the first license plate Jack's received. Back in January we were heading out to dinner one Friday night when Joe brought the mail in and plunked down a manila envelope addressed to Jack. Excitedly, Jack tore into it and pulled out a New York plate and a letter written on lined paper from Jacki, my former boss' wife, from Buffalo. In the letter she told Jack how she remembered him as a small baby, how her mother is still alive, how she doesn't like purple plaid skirts either. And he was thrilled.

About a month ago I was sitting on the beige couch in our psychologist, Phoebe's, office. (Phoebe is not her real name, by the way. But it's kind of close to her real name.)

(Actually, it's not even remotely close to her real name. I just like the sound of Phoebe; feee-beee. If I ever get a cat, I'm totally naming it Phoebe, even if it's a boy cat.)

Phoebe and I talked about some of the concerns Jack's working through right now: fire drills, bathroom issues, a slight rise in his anxiety. I mentioned how he's started writing notes to kids in school every day and signs them *from your secret admirer.* I told her about the inter-school mail system, where kids use multi-colored paper to pen letters and "mail them" to the classrooms. I admitted I was uncomfortable with Jack sending these messages. I fretted that he was making a spectacle of himself, that the other kids (and parents) might get annoyed with his daily correspondence. I worried these letters represented an inner world Jack had created for himself, an imaginary world of friendships and admiration.

Phoebe sat back in her chair and crossed her legs. "I don't know," she said slowly, thoughtfully. "I'm not sure we need to worry just yet." She explained this may just be Jack's way of endearing himself to his peers, of reaching out to them using an approach that makes him comfortable. And so I agreed to let it go for a while, to let the note-writing run its course. But I wasn't convinced.

And then, three days later, this note came home in his backpack. I share it with you in all its grade-school glory:

Dear Jack:

Hi, Jack. Can't wait for you to read out loud. I love choetle feaver do you? Send a letter back.

Your secret admirer.

Cute, right? (And before you ask, I have no idea what "choetle feaver" is.)

The day after Cynthia reached through the window of her Odyssey and handed me the license plate, school was canceled because of snow. Our area was hit twice; once in the morning, with the heavy snowflakes letting up for a few hours around noon, and then beginning again in earnest late in the afternoon. During the lull between storms I suggested to the kids that we head out for a quick lunch in town. They agreed, and in between shouts of *where's my coat* and *do I need boots* and *let's go to that place that has corn dogs*, Jack quietly disappeared into my home office. He emerged a few minutes later, a disc in hand, and asked me to play the CD during the ride to the restaurant. "It's an Easter CD," he said curtly when I asked what was on it.

Once in the car, I popped it in. I looked back in the rearview mirror and saw one of his rare gap-toothed grins. He was rocking and grunting in excitement. The first beats of a song started and Joey broke into a wide smile. "Hey! This is my favorite song!"

While the rest of us were bustling around the kitchen finding gloves and jackets and hats, Jack had logged onto iTunes, downloaded everyone's favorite song, and saved them to a disc. Each child cheered and shouted when they heard the music, and all the while Jack sat between Joey and Charlie in the third row of the van, silently rocking and smiling.

As we pulled into the parking lot of the restaurant, a special song for me began: "I Will Wait" by Mumford and Sons. Jack broke out of his reverie long enough to explain choppily, "Mom. It's your favorite. You like it."

And it is one of my favorites. Whenever I hear it I always think of Jack; the somewhat frantic, chaotic interplay of guitar and banjo, the phrases *use my head alongside my heart, paint my spirit gold*. And the hushed verse *I will wait, I will wait, for you.*

I think this song perfectly captures my own relationship with autism, of finding balance between holding back and pushing forward, of altering course or letting him steer. It reminds me of kneeling next to three-year-old Jack as he sat, unmoving, unblinking, in his stroller at the Buffalo Zoo, pointing and talking *look see the elephant so big Jack so big*, wondering when this boy was going to open his mind to the world so we could know him and he could know us.

Now, nearly five years later, he has done just that. With license plates and music and letters, Jack is connecting with the world on his terms. And the world is responding.

To all of you who have reached out to this boy of mine, who have dug old license plates out of your storage areas and expressed a shared disdain for purple plaid skirts, who have danced for just one moment to the beat of Jack's unusual music, I am forever your secret admirer.

A Few Words About S'Mores

Last summer we went to a friend's house for an end-of-season barbecue. To be honest, we sort of invited ourselves to said barbecue because we had gone the previous year and Jack—of course—remembered the exact date. So when he ran into my friend at the elementary school Meet-and-Greet, he demanded to know if we were coming to their party again this year.

And so my friend, lovely person that she is, sent an email the next day inviting us. And we, shameless people that we are, happily accepted. We love barbecues!

We arrived around 3 p.m. and there were about three dozen people in total, largely comprised of a collection of tweens and toddlers—and one sweet little newborn. For the entire afternoon the kids alternated between swimming and volleyball and riding bikes in the driveway, while the adults chatted and snacked on delicious appetizers like baked brie and stromboli. (Our friends are excellent cooks.)

Throughout the day I'd catch a glimpse of Jack here and there, running and laughing with other kids, throwing water balloons, riding the scooters, grabbing handfuls of chips. When an afternoon thunderstorm caught us all by surprise, he danced and giggled in the driveway with everyone else, shaking water from his hair and stepping barefoot in the puddles. At one point Joe and I caught each other's eyes and exchanged our he's-doing-so-well look.

After dinner everyone headed out into the wet yard to make s'mores in the somewhat soggy fire pit. I stood on the deck chatting with a woman about new puppies and watched as Jack meandered close to the circle of kids, reached into the plastic bag to grab a marshmallow, then skipped away, never staying put long enough to make a s'more for himself.

One by one the kids straggled away from the fire, gooey s'mores in hand. One by one, each family began to pack up and leave. *It's time to go find your sandals* I heard, and *say goodbye say thank you.*

Before we knew it, we were the last ones left, seated around the table amongst the half-empty water bottles and crumb-filled plates. (Note: When you invite yourself to a barbecue, you should always be the last to leave. It's in the etiquette manual. Look it up if you don't believe me.)

Joey came out and asked to go swimming again. I looked at Joe and he shrugged his shoulders. "Why not?" And off they went to find their still-damp bathing suits.

We sat relaxing on the deck in the waning light and watched the kids splash and jump in the brightly lit pool, swatting mosquitoes and swapping summer stories and back-to-school tales, when Jack suddenly charged up the steps towards the table. I noticed the stormy expression on his face and started to rise out of my chair to intercept him, but he launched himself at Joe instead.

"I want a s'more."

"No Jack. The s'mores are done for the night," Joe told him firmly. "The fire is out."

Our friend made a motion behind Jack's head, indicating he'd be happy to start the fire and make another, but we shook our heads *no no he will be fine it's time we got going.*

"NO! A s'more! I NEVER HAD ONE!"

"We'll make some tomorrow, buddy."

We decided that was our cue to head out. Joe herded the kids out of the pool, distributed towels, and shuttled them into the car while I bustled around the house collecting hastily discarded t-shirts and previously used towels.

"I WANT A S'MORE!"

Chewing on the end of his own towel, blue, his eyes glazed with anger, Jack listened while our friend told him he could be the first one back to use their fire pit in the spring, the first to roast a sticky marshmallow and squeeze it between two graham crackers.

All at once he flipped the towel forward and screamed, "NO! I am NEVER COMING BACK! I never want to SEE YOU AGAIN."

Joe propelled him to the car by the arm while my friend and I exchanged the usual *he's tired he's overwhelmed it's a lot to handle*. But still I had a pit in my stomach. The day felt ruined.

After returning home and settling the kids in bed, Joe and I sat on the couch for a while, indignant and righteous. Phrases like *if we'd ever done that as kids* and *he needs a consequence* were bandied around. We talked about taking away music, the computer, iTunes, but none of those felt connected enough to the behavior.

As we headed up to bed, I suggested we make him apologize.

"He can either write an email or call, but he has to acknowledge how rude he was." Joe turned to look at me as we climbed the stairs and said, "And we'll tell him how proud we are once he says he's sorry."

This morning I woke early to the sound of heavy rain. I lay next to Joe and listened to his light snoring, thinking about all the things we need to teach Jack, all the things that are not intuitive to him. Regulation and empathy and regret. Contrition and forgiveness and impulse control.

Although he pictures the days as color, Jack's mind works in black and white, in absolutes: *I was angry. I wanted a s'more. At this moment, these people will not give me a s'more so I NEVER WANT TO SEE THEM AGAIN.* These are the words he reaches for in moments of stress and chaos and anger.

I have a tendency to want to wrap autism up in sparkly paper and tie it with a large, satin bow and present it to the world. *See world?* Isn't autism *fun* and *interesting* and *unique* and *extraordinary*?

And it is. It is all of those things. But there is also this abrupt side, a rude side, an *unlikable* side that doesn't sparkle no matter what kind of wrapping paper you use.

These instances force me to stretch myself. Sitting here at my desk with my cup of coffee on this rainy morning, I badly want to let it go, to say *he's just a kid, kids are rude, they are our friends and they understand.*

But then an image rises unbidden to my mind, an image of thirty-year-old Jack barking at a colleague or a girlfriend or a neighbor, telling them he never wants to see them again over something as trivial as an unmade s'more.

And so I will dig a little deeper to teach the lessons of *manners* and *behavior*, while at the same time trying to respect the confines of his spectrum disorder, the limits of his expressive language. To respect that beneath the missing graham cracker and melted chocolate and gooey marshmallow are real feelings of loss, of anger, of shame.

In the end, he chose to write a text.

> *Hi it's Jack. I feel sad about yesterday. I am sorry. I had fun and you have a nice pool but it's cold. Last time we visited your house was September 1 2012.*

Joe read it over and turned to his son, "Jack, we are so proud of you. We are proud."

Holding up the Bus: A How-To Guide for Getting What You Want

"I have a question," said a woman in the second row. She was wearing a red cardigan and had been quiet for most of the hour. "How do you get the things you want from the school?"

I was finishing up a reading in a nearby town and the discussion had just about petered out. Out of the corner of my eye I could see the next author leafing through the novel she'd written, preparing her notes and looking at her watch.

"Uh, good question!" I stammered. "Well, we kind of all work together. As a team. You know, we've never really had a problem getting what Jack needs to, you know, to do well."

The woman in red nodded. My answer was unconvincingly lame and I'm pretty sure she knew it. But before I could go any further the bookstore owner shot forward and wrapped things up.

I've thought about her question off and on for the past month; how *do* I get the things I want from the school?

To answer this requires more than a two-minute response, the amount of time most post-reading questions allow for.

It deserves more of an answer, more thought. After doing that thinking I can sum it up with three separate, seemingly unrelated anecdotes about an imaginary play date, door knobs, and grief.

Bear with me.

Back when Jack was in first grade, he watched as second-grade Joey took the bus to different friends' houses for play dates each week. He expressed interest in a play date himself, which is to say he told us, "I want play. To take the bus."

One afternoon he decided to take matters into his own hands and followed a little blonde girl onto her bus because he was going to "sleep at her house." You know, without packing a bag or telling anyone first or even knowing the girl's last name.

That same afternoon I had some friends over for lunch, and over the din of babies and toddlers and laughter, I never heard the school call the house to find out if he had a note or if he was supposed to take another bus home.

Between the missed call and an irate six-year-old with autism, there was a fair amount of dismissal-time chaos at school. Eventually they reached Joe, who raced over to pick him up, but in the meantime all of the buses were delayed while Jack screamed and thrashed.

Once everyone was home, Joey—visibly shaken—relayed the scene through his then eight-year-old eyes: "Mom, he was screaming and crying. They couldn't calm him down. All the buses had to wait and everyone was looking at him."

This was on a Friday afternoon so I had the entire

weekend to seethe, to simmer, to fret. I was outraged. For two days I ranted against the injustice, the unfairness, the discrimination of it all; no one should make a spectacle of my son. They embarrassed him! They humiliated Joey! Why couldn't they have brought him back into the school, let the buses go, and saved everyone such an ugly scene?

As soon as the kids boarded the bus Monday morning, I installed Henry and Rose in front of *Mickey Mouse Playhouse* and called the school. I was connected with the vice principal and shakily, with a weekend's worth of tension behind my voice, asked what happened. And right away she said something unforgettable.

"Mrs. Cariello," she answered. "We could have done better."

Sitting at my desk in my bathrobe I could hear Rose's raspy voice counting to ten in unison with Goofy, and I closed my eyes against a rush of tears. All at once, my fortress of rage and indignation crumbled to the floor, brick by angry brick.

"Thank you," I whispered. "That was all I needed to hear." And I realized it was.

For the rest of the morning I thought about the idea of *doing better*, and as I poured Cheerios and changed diapers, my mind wandered back to when Jack was about four years old.

He'd just started what I like to call his Door Clicking Phase. For about six months he moved steadily throughout the house all day, twisting each door knob and clicking the door open and closed and opened and closed to test who knows what—how many times he could do it, maybe? How hard he needed to push before the door opened? It drove me to the brink of sanity. I had a newborn and a kindergartener at the time, and all sorts of small people scattered in between. If there was ever a time for door-clicking, this was *not* it.

One day I reached my breaking point. We were in the kitchen and I was trying to get him to put his shoes on so I could pick his older brother up before his younger brother needed to nurse and his middle brother peed in his pirate costume because we were potty training. I was holding blue Stride Rite sneakers in one hand and asking four-year-old Jack over and over *listen to Mommy put your sneakers on here are your sneakers put them on*. He wouldn't even look at me, lost to an inner world of door knobs.

Click. Click. Click.

And people, I kid you not when I tell you I dropped those sneakers to the floor, grabbed fistfuls of my own hair with my own hands, and jumped up and down begging—BEGGING—this boy at the top of my lungs to *stop stop STOP that clicking right now before I lose my mind STOP IT*.

Trust me when I say this: I COULD HAVE DONE BETTER.

(Note: The Door-Clicking Phase was immediately followed by the Toilet-Top-Removal Phase. After watching Joe lift the top of the tank off the toilet one afternoon to look for whatever it is men look for in the back of the toilet, Jack would spend the day going from bathroom to bathroom, trying to slide the heavy porcelain lid off himself. And following that came one of my favorites: the Smearing-of-Bath-and-Body-Works-Anti-Bacterial-Foam-Soap-All-Over-the-Walls Phase.)

A few months ago our school's special education department held a meeting to talk about some changes in their program, plans to make the integration room more soothing and the classroom transitions easier. When the presentation finished, hands started to wave and angry voices began to fill the air, asking *what about those iPads you promised* and *why can't we have the same aide as last year* and *how long before we see any real change.*

All at once the room felt emotionally charged, tense. I leaned back in my chair and closed my eyes against the conflict. As the angry dialogue rose and fell around me, I heard a quieter subtext, a softer voice struggling to be heard: *she is not talking he is not learning I am scared I am scared help me.*

I heard grief.

Grief is such a funny thing, isn't it? It rears its sad little face in a variety of ways, and before you know it something like *I am terrified because my child has autism* becomes *everyone is wrong we are not getting what we want we need more.* Before you know it, that sad face contorts and twists into an expression of rage.

We parents of special needs kiddos are constantly grieving: grieving the loss of a child who may never have a play date, who may never speak, who is simply never going to be the son or daughter we imagined when the nurse first placed that tiny bundle in our arms so long ago. But over the years I have learned I have to open my own fragile heart and let other people see how raw and tender it all is, how I bleed for my son who follows a little girl at dismissal because he wants to sleep at her house, how I die a little each day when I watch him through the bus windows, stimming and zooming, eventually taking a seat. By himself.

I have learned to say *I don't know what to do he will this is so hard I am failing I need you.* To say *I cannot do this alone.*

And beautifully, magically, the teachers and paraprofessionals and principals reach back. They wear glasses to school. They say "I can." They *do better.*

And they do this even though Jack isn't the only student at school. He isn't even the only special needs student, or even the only student with autism. He isn't always going to get a fancy iPad or extra time in speech therapy.

But that doesn't mean he can hold up the bus.

Because it's not so much getting what you want as it is accepting what people can give. Tolerance, compassion, acceptance—those are the unlimited resources that promote progress and change, that help a small boy learn to read and write and regulate and play.

That's what I wish I'd told the woman in the red sweater.

I'd like to thank every teacher who has wept along with me when I panicked that Jack wasn't making progress, who handed me a tissue and assured me *we aren't giving up he will learn to read.* Who accepted his thirty million secret admirer letters with grace and counted how many times he went to the bathroom to make sure he didn't have a stomach ache he couldn't find the words to describe. Who held his hand during fire drills and patiently, oh so patiently, coaxed words from his silent lips.

Because in the end, these are the things I want.

Vacation Pictures

A young guy wearing a light pink Oxford shirt with the sleeves rolled up walked over to where Joe and I were sitting at the bar and plunked down on the stool next to me. "Hey guys! How are you?"

"Well, hello!" Joe said back. "How are you?"

That afternoon, after two planes and a harrowing bus ride that made the phrase "until death do us part" more meaningful than ever, Joe and I arrived at the heaven on earth that is Jamaica.

We exchanged a few pleasantries with our new friend—soon realizing the gin and tonic he ordered wasn't his first of the night—and asked what had brought him to Negril, the small beach town on the west end of the island where we were staying.

"My sister, she's getting married here tomorrow. I can't believe she's getting married," he said, incredulous.

"She's eight years older than I am and she's getting *married*. I mean, I could be a nephew! How crazy is that?"

"I think," I corrected him gently, "You would be an *uncle*."

"Yes! That's right! I could be an uncle. Can you believe it? My sister is getting married *tomorrow*."

The conversation ended as quickly as it started, and before we knew it he was up from the bar, clapping both Joe and I heartily on the shoulder. "I'll see you later, okay guys?"

Maybe it was because I'd finished Anna Quindlen's *Still Life With Bread Crumbs* on the plane ride—a novel about a woman photographer—but I wanted to take pictures the entire time we were on vacation. Not just of the stunning sunsets or the sparkling ocean or of Joe enjoying a Red Stripe, but of the startling images of color and depth we saw everywhere: a small red boat buried halfway in the sand, a large brown dog lying in the tall grass, an emaciated man selling sundries in the street on the long ride from the airport.

On Tuesday we went down the beach to the Fireman, a man who sold and prepared fresh seafood. Everyone raved about him; you picked your own crab or lobster from the big cage he dragged out of the water, and then he grilled it right in front of you.

Joe and I walked over to the wooden porch and sat at a picnic table to wait while the Fireman whistled and hummed and cooked. Locals drifted in and out, grabbing cold bottles of beer and trading good-natured insults with the bartender and the tourists.

After a few minutes a little girl wearing a green bathing suit toddled out of the kitchen area. At first glance I guessed she was about two, but very tiny for her age. Her mother walked behind her, waving her finger and speaking quick lively bursts of Jamaican patois.

I gazed back at them, watching the scene of mother chasing toddler unfold. The rest of the family appeared, followed soon after by a trail of older kids weaving in and around the chairs and talking to each other.

I looked across the table and caught Joe's eye, and he gave a quick nod. Yes, he saw what I saw; the little girl appeared to have Down Syndrome.

I felt my heart pull. What are the services like in Jamaica? Would she get speech therapy? Occupational therapy? On the bus ride to the resort we passed school after school, small, squat buildings with throngs of uniformed children mingling with goats on the patchy grass. Somehow I couldn't imagine that the services this girl needed were readily available.

Just then one of the older boys—eleven or twelve I guessed—strode across the wooden floorboards, breaking me out of my reverie. In one smooth movement, he bent down and picked the little girl up.

Watching his wide smile as he lifted her high above his own head made me want to weep, and I'd never wanted to take a picture so badly in my life. But to whip out my iPhone and pose them seemed a crude interruption of the moment at hand—even though the moment doubtlessly repeats itself over and over throughout the day.

Can you see him? Can you picture this lanky boy bending to lift this small girl? He holds her face close to his while she squirms and giggles. They are framed by the wooden pillars of the porch, the ocean a glimmering blue behind them.

If you see it—if you can picture them in your mind's eye—then I know you're feeling the exquisite combination of love and tenderness explode inside your heart that I did. It is almost painful.

For me, the quick swing of a brother's long, thin arms changed the story from *class* and *services* and *who will write her individualized education program* into a universal account of *compassion* and *family* and *special* and *needs*. It turned into a story of a sibling's love, a love not at all different from the love Jack's siblings have for him.

Watching them, it occurred to me that all this time—more than two years of writing and speaking—I've been trying to do exactly this, to give to you a picture of our family and of our kids and of our autism.

But I can't take a picture of Jack's autism and put it in an album or post it on Facebook. Sure, I can photograph his downturned eyes and his vacant expression and even catch him stimming. But I can't capture the social awkwardness, the obsession with the Keurig, the *I don't want this autism in me anymore*.

A photo may show you how autism *looks*, but it won't tell you how it *feels*. I can only begin to guess about that.

Two days later Joe and I were sharing a late lunch at an outdoor café on the resort. As we finished up, a couple walked over and ordered a drink. I recognized them from the destination wedding a few days before—the bride and groom. We chatted about their wedding: the beautiful weather, how she'd added the belt to her dress at the last minute.

"Well," she said, nodding in the direction of the portrait studio behind them. "Time to look at wedding pictures!"

"Oh, wait!" I put my hand on her arm as she turned away, remembering. "We met your brother!"

She turned back to me. "*George*? You met George? Oh boy, what did he say?" she asked warily.

"He was so happy for you," I told her. "It was the sweetest thing—he was in awe of your getting married. He hopes he'll be an uncle soon."

The new bride looked up at her tall groom. Her eyes widened and her face flushed pink.

"He said all that? I can't believe he told you that. I have to tell my father, it will make him so happy."

For the second time in as many days, I watched a powerful family moment of adaptation and change, shifting and movement—of brotherly love.

My fingers itched for my iPhone. I longed to take a picture and turn the small screen towards her and say, "Do you see how beautiful you are? Do you see what you look like when you realize how much your brother adores you?"

But I didn't.

We left the next day, and on the plane ride back I scrolled through the pictures I had taken on my phone. I decided I will never become a photographer. The dog looked hot and tired. The red boat looked ordinary. The sunset looked nice, but really, who can't take a nice picture of a sunset?

I leaned my head back and closed my eyes, my mind wandering back to the little girl in her green bathing suit. I smiled remembering the way her diaper poked out of the bottom, how her pigtails were a little uneven. And I decided she would be just fine. Maybe she wouldn't get *early intervention* or *modified homework* or *organized social play*, but her family loves her. Sometimes that's all you need.

Best vacation ever.

The Person I'm With Has Autism

"Hey Carrie, it's me, Sandy. Listen, I had an idea for you." Sandy is a dog trainer. We started to work with her after we got Wolfie because we have no idea what we're doing.

"Oh, I'm so glad you called! I'm kind of worried he doesn't like his food. He isn't eating it as fast. And when he chews it he kind of makes a funny face, you know? Like he—"

"I'm not talking about Wolfie," she cut in impatiently. "I'm reading your book and—"

"You are? That's so nice! Did you get to the part about dogs? I know, it's so sad because Wolfie isn't in it. But we didn't have him yet! Maybe I should write a new book, just about him. I could call it The Wolfman. Or Wolferoni, that's kind of his nick—"

"No, it's not about dogs," she said brusquely. "I'm reading the chapter where you say you wish you had some kind of sign to tell people about Jack and his autism."

In my first book, I wrote a chapter called "Sign," where I

talked about how I wished there was a universal hand signal to let people know Jack has autism.

Sandy went on to explain how she takes care of her mother, who has Alzheimer's, and how the Alzheimer's Association issues family members little business cards they can give to people at the hair salon or the grocery store or the library.

"They say, '*The person I'm with has Alzheimer's. Please be patient.*' This way, my mother doesn't have to feel self-conscious and I can help people understand her a little better."

"Huh. That *is* a good idea," I said thoughtfully. I went back to chatting about puppy food and house training, and although I didn't forget the business card idea altogether, I didn't think much more about it. Until we took a family vacation.

Because we hate ourselves, this past June Joe and I decided to take the kids to Texas.

(Note: For those of you who have never been, it's hot in Texas. It's really hot in June. In fact, the Texas heat in June makes the Bikram yoga hot room feel like you need a sweater. It's death hot. I-can't-breathe hot. Someone-turn-off-the-sun hot.)

But while we may hate ourselves, we love Joe's sister, Elaine. And Elaine lives in Texas. So for the second year in a row we packed up five children and four suitcases, braved airport security, and headed west.

Excited beyond measure, Jack filled his carry-on with his usual favorites: his stuffed bunny and moose-shaped pillow, nasal spray, and ChapStick. Like always, he also brought his rigidness and bossiness and *how many more minutes*-ness.

He also brought the deepest, most awful sounding cough you've ever heard in your life. It sounded like a cross between croup and a chainsaw. And he is the worst cougher you've ever seen.

I know, I know, kids cough, right? They get colds and they cough and sometimes—gasp—they don't even cover their mouths! But Jack takes coughing to a whole new level. Something to do with that whole controlling your body thing. He jumps and flails and throws his head back. He *amplifies*.

Three times I brought him to the doctor's for antibiotics and inhaler thingies and new recommendations for cough medicine. Three times the doctor promised me that it wasn't whooping cough or bronchitis or the plague, and that we were safe to travel. So last Monday morning at 4:30, the seven of us were off.

Fast-forward two hours later, with all of us seated at a table in Johnny Rockets at Boston's Logan Airport, kicking off our trip with greasy hash browns and sticky pancakes. Cue tremendous coughing fit. A woman and her son, who had nodded and smiled pleasantly at us just moments before, picked up their trays and moved three tables away.

"JACK! Cover your *mouth*! And *sit down*!"

"I can't. I can't. I don't know what my body is doing."

And when he wasn't coughing, he was busy being, well, Jack. A few minutes later we were jostling our way to the gate when he collided with a security man. "HEY!" Jack screamed at him. "Watch where you are GOING! That was RUDE."

"JACK!" I turned to the man. "So sorry. He didn't mean that! Sorry. He's, um, well, he gets overwhelmed."

As we boarded the plane I thought about Sandy's suggestion for business cards. Settling into my seat, I considered a few ideas and giggled to myself:

Someone I'm with has autism. Guess who?

Someone I'm with has autism. Now hand me a drink.

Someone I'm with has autism. Please do not mention anything about toilets or spiders or Wyoming.

Next to me Jack boomed, "What are you LAUGHING ABOUT? Have you seen what kind of toilets they have on this AIRPLANE?"

When Jack was just a little guy, I could smile and announce, "He's on the autism spectrum," as loudly as I wanted. He had no idea. But now he's ten, and he knows. And he doesn't like the label.

So there's no announcing it anymore. Now I kind of shift my head to one side and mumble something like, "He's, um, you know." Sometimes, for no reason I can explain, I clear my throat.

But they *don't* know. That's the thing. They look over at him and glance back at me and there's just a lot of confusion.

For the rest of our trip I thought about how maybe business cards really were the answer. It would save everyone a lot of awkwardness, like when Jack asked the server at Friendly's if her mother was still alive, or wondered out loud in the middle of SeaWorld, "What does PIT HAIR FEEL LIKE?"

He was standing next to a man with no shirt on at the time.

A business card could promote tolerance and acceptance. It could make the world love autism. Most of all, it could save my son from the embarrassment of such an announcement.

Oh! I almost forgot to tell you what else Jack brought on our Texan vacation. That would be his latest fixation. And what is that latest fixation, you ask? Black widow spiders or license plates or birthdays or toilets? Nope. Nothing as cute and endearing as all that.

Right now, he's fascinated with—wait for it—Nazi Germany.

At the airport in Austin, Jack and I stopped for some water and gum while we waited for our plane to board. Just as I handed my credit card over to the young twenty-something behind the kiosk, Jack blurted out, "Did you KNOW. Annie Frank died when she was fifteen." The guy blinked at him and looked back at me. I cleared my throat.

"JACK!" I whisper-shouted as we walked away. "Don't ask people about that if we don't know them. And it's *Anne* Frank, not Annie."

"It has an 'E'," he said stubbornly. "So it's Ann-*ee*. The concentration camps. Did they have campfires?"

Suddenly I felt very tired. As we stepped on the moving concourse, I closed my eyes against the naiveté of it all; the absurdity of a boy who has the emotional maturity of maybe a six-year-old trying to grasp the horror of a concentration camp. The absurdities of pit hair and coughing and even autism.

Standing next to Jack, I realized it's not the lingering gazes or the small stares or even the occasional child's pointed finger that I mind. I don't. It's that people don't know him.

I think more than wanting people to know something about today's autism buzzwords, words like *tolerance* and *acceptance* and *embrace what is different* and *blah blah blah*, I just want the world to know *him*.

Trust me, I realize this is a lot to ask, especially since I myself often fail to see beneath autism's tough exterior to the little boy hiding underneath. It's certainly a lot to ask of a two-inch by three-inch piece of cardstock.

But I want people—I want *you*—to know that he is so very funny. And interesting. And smart. And rude and abrupt and curious and innocent and scared. He is trying his best to master a difficult world, to understand manners and to cover his mouth when he coughs, to use polite words and to keep his body still. But I don't know how to fit all of that on a business card.

Someone I'm with has autism. Please give him a chance and try not to judge him. This will be hard.

Someone I'm with has autism. He might ask you a lot of weird questions but he just wants to know more about you.

Someone I'm with has autism. He is doing the best he can.

On the flight home Joe sat next to Jack. I relaxed back

in my seat, glad for the four-hour respite from the hacking cough and the stimming and the "Annie" Frank. About half-way to New Hampshire, Joe reached over and tapped my shoulder. I looked up from my Nook, startled.

"Jack just told me he prays to God every night. He prays He'll take his autism away."

I cleared my throat. And as I turned back around, I thought of the perfect card:

Someone I'm with has autism. It's complicated.

This is What a Bajillion Looks Like

One day I was standing in the cramped lobby of the gym, chatting with another dad and waiting for Henry's Tiny Tots tumbling class to end. As we talked about our three-year-olds and kids in general, I mentioned that I have a son with autism. "Oh," he said with an interested expression on his kind face. "What kind of autism does he have?"

I stammered for a moment and tried to think of how to explain Jack and his autism, but just then the weary-looking gymnastics instructor opened the door and released our exuberant preschoolers. The father and I were distracted with putting socks and sneakers on squirming chubby feet, and I never did answer him.

I am no stranger to questions—since Jack was a squirrely toddler fixating on vacuums and barely speaking, people have asked me what was wrong with him, will he get better, will he talk. Through the years complete strangers have asked me what it's like to live with someone who can remember the exact dates he ate hot dogs during 2009. For the most part these queries are well-intentioned, and I've never minded answering any of them.

But in eight years I've never been asked such a beautifully poignant question, and I considered it for the entire drive home: What kind of autism *does* Jack have? I wasn't really sure. And then I wondered: what kind of autism does *Jack* think he has?

We know he knows he has it. And we know he hates it. But what does it mean to him, exactly?

So I conducted some high-level research. It went something like this:

Me: "Jack, what does autism mean to you?"

Jack (ears covered, face screwed up): "Stop TALKING about this to me."

Me: "But what do you think it means to have—"

Jack: "NO MORE TALKING."

So I had to go underground with my investigation, resorting to strict observation, examining and noting his reactions in various situations.

As best as I can understand, Jack thinks autism means you earn things.

Let me give you an example. Last week I had to bring Jack to yet another eye appointment. The appointment was at 12:45 p.m. We needed an hour and fifteen minutes to get there, which meant we needed to leave by 11:30. This left me plenty of time to take a 9 a.m. Crossfit class, go home, shower, and then head over to pick Jack up from school.

There was just one minor autism-related snafu: Jack remembered that the last time we went for an eye appointment in Boston—on Tuesday, December 10th at 10:30 a.m. and the doctor wore a black dress and we were in the exam room with light blue walls—he stayed home from school all day. And so now he wanted to stay home again.

This did not parse well with my plans for working out. But, I have experience with this kind of thing. I know what I'm doing. I've read all the books and done all the research about child rearing and autism and parenting, and so I did what every good mother would do in this situation. I reached for the bribe.

"Jack, if you go I will buy you *Snow White* on DVD."

"The Disney Special Platinum Edition or the Two-Disc Extended Edition?"

"Uh, whichever one you want," I told him, making a mental note to limit his time on Amazon.

"NO! That is EARNING! I won't EARN A DVD. People with autism earn things."

You see? He has somehow gotten the idea that having autism means you have to earn things. It should be fun trying to convince him to get a job someday. He may very well believe that everyone who has one also has autism. Else why would they do it?

When we first started talking to Jack about his autism, we tried to explain it in terms he could understand. We told him his mind works differently and sometimes his body moves because of something called *self-stimulation*, what he sometimes hears us call "stimming."

Naturally, he had a lot of questions. He wondered if he could die from it and why he has it and if he'll ever get rid of it. He also asked, "Who else. Has autism."

We kind of skipped over that one.

Then one day last spring he came off the bus and said, "I

am the only one. In my class with autism." And that afternoon it dawned on me: he feels alone in the spectrum world.

Sure, I can tell him all about the statistics. I could sit him down and say, "Listen, Jack, one out of sixty-eight kids are diagnosed now, so there are literally a bajillion people like you, people who picture Wednesday as orange and remember what the ophthalmologist wore six months ago." But somehow, even though Jack lives for details and numbers just like these, I didn't think it would make a difference in the most important way, in his *understanding*. Still, it was clear that he was trying to do just that, to figure out what autism *was*.

"Henry. Henry has autism," Jack announced one afternoon. We'd just finished picking blueberries and I looked over at my youngest—who was trying to see if one of the ripened berries would fit in his nostril—and then back at Jack.

"I can see why you might think that," I said slowly. "But he isn't diagnosed with autism."

"Who else. Who else has it."

"Well, lots of people have autism, Jack."

"WHO!"

What do I say? Of course I know other kids who have it, adults even. But it is not my place to open that dialogue. So instead, I try to point out autism's more savory qualities, things like Jack's memory and his kindness, his determination and his progress. But it does little to abate the obvious loneliness, the isolation of being the only one in his family, in his class, of feeling like maybe the only one in the universe diagnosed with spectrum disorder.

It's as though I'm telling him this: *Jack you are a brilliant unicorn amongst us ordinary horses. You are so beautiful! We know there are tons of you out there—bajillions, even—but we don't know how to show you. We don't know where they all are.* Oh, and magical unicorn? We don't really get you. We don't understand you. We are blinded by your colorful beauty but your tantrums scare the crap out of us. In fact, maybe it would just be better if you were a plain old horse like the rest of us. Then we could figure out how to teach you fractions.

For a while now Jack's been telling me he wants his autism to stay a secret. He wants to keep it from the teachers and principal and students in middle school. As of yet, I have not had the heart—or the courage—to tell him they already know, that things called *IEP* and *paraprofessionals* and a *modified course load* have been in the works for a while.

I never had a concrete plan or vision when I started writing, but it's been over two years now, and looking back I guess I did it, at least in part, so I would feel less alone. From the safety of my little office I could share my heartache and make my jokes and connect through cyberspace with other people like me who are also balancing autism and parenthood and math homework and swimming lessons. And if there was a smidgen of autism awareness to the whole thing, well, that was just a bonus.

But ultimately, I have failed. I have failed because, while I feel connected to a wider community of people, the boy sitting in the room next to me—the boy with autism—feels confused and scared and ashamed.

He feels alone.

More than that, he wants to hide something that is as fundamental and essential to him as his beating heart or his thinking brain or the freckle on his right forearm. He wants to keep autism a secret.

I wish to somehow show him that there are, in fact, a bajillion more people like him in this world. That there are boys and girls and fathers and daughters who cover their ears during fireworks and squint against fluorescent lighting's blinding glare. People who have individualized education programs and aides in the classroom, who love license plates and calendars and Katy Perry, and who battle anxiety's fierce snake. I want to show him that many of those same people play beautiful music and have jobs and love to go to the movies and always eat ice cream after dinner.

That they are, in essence, just like him.

And so I reached out to my own community—to my neighbors both real and virtual, to the tens of thousands of people out there who have taken an interest in my son—in order to expand Jack's solitary world. I asked people to go to my Facebook page and post the name of someone they know with autism, and to share as much or as little as they wanted to.

To share the name and age of a son or daughter or neighbor or student or brother (or maybe even themselves). To share a picture if they felt comfortable. And, if they could, to add a little note, something that makes these people special.

I even went first.

My son Jack has autism. He is ten. He is as magical as a unicorn.

I was simply blown away by the hundreds and hundreds and hundreds of responses. I expected the posts to look like this:

Owen, 11, New York.

But instead, people wrote things like this:

Hey, Jack. This is my son, also named Jack. He has autism. He is seven years old. And, although his social skills are deemed "very poor," you'll never meet a human being with a greater ability to "own the room." You are not alone, my friend.

I read each and every message, email, comment, and post. I read them and I re-read them and when I was done with that, I read them all again. I cried every time.

Joe does not handle the crying well. He does not know what to do when I cry. He kind of clears his throat and looks down at his feet, bewildered. Eventually he offers me a cookie. This usually works, and I stop.

But I could not stop because people kept writing. They wrote stories about their favorite people and how much they love Minecraft and Legos and spaceships and pirates. They posted pictures.

Hello, Jack! This is my fifteen-year-old grandson, who also has autism. He is the wonderful unicorn in my world.

I saw Jack in their words. I saw myself in their words. I breathed in hope and encouragement, pain and love.

And the comments from the dads? Well, they simply dissolved me. I think it's because I know how much it would take for Joe to share about his son on a blog or in a

Facebook message, to reveal the pain and hope and fear that is unique to a father's heart.

> *I have a son who is fourteen and has autism. . . . I am a very athletic person and like most fathers looked forward to teaching and playing sports with my son which I cannot do. But what I can do is embrace the brilliant mind that my son has, his sense of humor, his kindness and his willingness to love—my job in life is to make sure Vinny can live the best life possible.*

Friends from high school reconnected. Old colleagues reached out, and one mother shared this about her quiet child's beautiful smile:

> *Hi Jack. My son has autism. He is six. He doesn't speak at all and he has a smile that can light up a room . . . just like yours.*

Teachers from around the country spoke:

> *I've had several students with autism and each one of them has changed my life in some way.*

Minnesota, New Jersey, Oregon, Illinois, California.

> *Hi Jack! Guess what? I have two sons who have autism. They are twins. They are thirteen years old and live in Iowa. One boy loves to go swimming, he loves elevators, and he has always enjoyed watching doors open and close. The other has a spectacular memory (he knows many facts), he sings with perfect pitch, and he plays the trombone.*

We read one message from a family in the Netherlands together over dinner at our favorite Mexican restaurant, watching as Jack's face lit with a slow smile. And then he reported, "Amsterdam. Is the capital of the Netherlands."

My younger son is autistic. He is eight and likes to play soccer and loves everything Minecraft. He is kind, loving and so much fun. We live in Iceland. You are not alone!

A few courageously shared a piece of themselves.

I have autism. I have a very successful life and I have my share of autism-related problems, too. But I'm twenty-five years old, I've accomplished much, and I love who I am. He is most definitely not alone.

Throughout the week Jack asked to read the comments. Watching his face light from within, I could tell that you did what I could not. Through words and sentences and paragraphs and social media, you connected my son to a larger world beyond himself.

You showed him that, yes, there are other magical unicorns.

My beautiful eleven-year-old has autism and ADHD; she too feels alone even when she's with others.

Many posts about your tender little toddlers reminded me of the days when Joe and I were in the trenches of autism, fighting the early signs. Right now we live with autism, we struggle and sometimes rejoice with autism, but that's nothing compared to the heat of the diagnosis battle, when you're trying to figure out services and early intervention and speech therapy, all while your little guy or gal is tearing up the house and starting the car.

I remember.

If I've learned anything from the responses, it's that autism casts a wide, arbitrary net. Sometimes the net scoops up more than one from a family, other times it is a solitary selection.

> *I have not one but two wonderful boys on the spectrum. . . . Autism is just a facet of who they are, like having brown eyes or blonde hair or freckles or skinny legs or glasses . . .*

After dinner one night this week, I sat down at my laptop for a few minutes to read everything over again, and to start putting my notes together for this chapter. Predictably, Jack came in to hover over my shoulder, begging for iTunes. But instead he was once again drawn into the thread on Facebook, to the pictures and details and descriptions of your daughters and sons, students and grandchildren, nephews and neighbors. And then he paused for a moment at a familiar name.

"Joe. Cariello," he breathed. "That is Dad."

I squinted at the screen and saw this all the way at the bottom of the Facebook thread:

> *Hi Jack. My son has autism, and I have loved you since the day you were born.*

Jack bounded out of the room to take his shower, and I sat in our little office thinking about how I just sent this one small request out into the universe and all of you, the universe, answered back.

I guess all this time I thought *bajillion* was just a number, a fictitious way to quantify replies. But I was wrong. It's not a number at all.

Bajillion is confusion and fear and golden dogs named Scooby. It is boys from Michigan and girls from Utah and a thirteen-year-old with perfect pitch. It is rage and disappointment, grace and unity. It is facing each other across the dinner table night after night with the same pit in your stomach while your son screams and thrashes on the floor because the squash is *too yellow too yellow too yellow*. It is Disney movies and breathtaking memory and the extraordinary gift of unusual people.

It is siblings sliding down autism's slippery bell curve together, laughing and giggling and looking up to the bright blue sky overhead.

Every Book Needs A "Resources" Section

In *What Color is Monday?* I added a small "Resources" section at the back of the book, mostly because it seemed like all books on autism had one, and because publishers like that sort of thing. And it was pretty useful, I suppose. It helps to have certain terms defined and to have the websites where you can get support, especially if you're new to this strangely beautiful world and feeling lost and alone. But when I came near the end of this book, and I thought about once more defining things like *theory of mind* and *individualized education program*, or of listing website addresses easily available through any Google search, it occurred to me that, well, I'd done that already. What I hadn't yet done was put together a list of those *other* resources, the ones that are less about the big issues and more about what a lot of us really need: advice on how to make the most out of each day while living with someone on the spectrum.

So, in no particular order, the following are my top

resources for living life with autism. I recommend them very, very highly.

Exercise

It took me a year to figure out how to do a double-under. You know, when you jump rope and you have to make the rope pass twice under your feet in a single jump? A whole year.

Lately I've been getting up at 6:00 a.m. to exercise because my Crossfit gym doesn't understand that I also have elements of autism and am extremely rigid about my schedule, and they went and canceled the 7:00 a.m. class I'd been taking forever.

It stinks. It really does. It stinks to get up when it's dark and cold out and it stinks to have to go to bed early worrying about my workout the next day.

But once I'm there I don't have to think about anything more than a rope passing under my feet five, ten, fifteen times in a row. All I have to do is listen to the steady *tick tick tick* of the rope hitting the floor and the deep exhales of my own breath and the blood rushing in my ears.

And suddenly it doesn't stink anymore.

A Good Babysitter

Obviously, it wasn't easy to find the right sitter who could handle five kids at a time, one of whom stims and has a verbal tic and obsesses about the color of the water in the toilet. But now we have several, and they love him and he loves them and the kids get excited and it's really great.

As I've mentioned, Joe and I have gone out on a "date"

every Saturday night since our oldest was six-months old. I can count on one hand the number of times we've missed our night out, and it was usually because I was in the hospital having another baby. And when we had a newborn, that little addition just came right along with us.

It's expensive to go out every week, plus sometimes I just don't feel like going. There are nights when I just want to crawl into a pair of pajamas and lie on the couch with a big bowl of ice cream.

But my truth is this: there are moments I worry our marriage will not make it. We have stresses like any other family and, on top of that, the stresses of having a kiddo on the spectrum. Date night revives us. We eat and we laugh and we talk about all sorts of funny things. We talk about fear. And I look in my husband's brown eyes and I think about how he's just as handsome and interesting as the day I met him.

And—bonus!—he always picks up the check.

Ghirardelli Brownies

Sometimes, I eat my feelings.

This habit started a year ago, when Jack was in third grade and homework really overwhelmed us both. Every couple of days I would bake a pan of brownies. You know, *for the kids*. And as the homework wars raged on throughout the course of the afternoon, I would begin picking the edges off until all that was left was a floating island of chocolate in the middle of the pan.

I figure I deserve it after all those dumb double-unders.

My Gut

Personally, I hate the word *gut*. It's ugly. But mine has never steered me wrong. I started following it when Jack was about six months old because it kept nagging at me and saying really annoying things like *wow he isn't doing things on time something is wrong*. It would not be silenced, even by the aforementioned brownies.

And so I began insisting we needed help, he needed help, and eventually, someone listened.

Family Pictures

I don't mean pictures of my family hanging on the walls. Who needs those? With the invention of the iPhone and digital photography, these kids have been taking selfies and posting them all over my screens for a year now.

No, I'm talking about a book here: *Family Pictures* by Sue Miller.

Right now you're probably thinking Aha! A book! Finally, something I can sink my teeth into on this silly list of "resources."

Except its fiction. It's about a family with six kids, and the second son, Randall, has a severe form of autism. I first read it when I was in college and I've probably re-read it every year or so since.

It isn't even so much about Randall, as much as it's about how the entire family breaks down around him—in many ways because of him—due to the tremendous stress a kiddo with autism can place on a family. The parents disconnect. They divorce. The kids resent Randall. It's kind of a mess and there really isn't a happy ending. (Or maybe there is. I don't want to spoil it for you.) In some ways, it is my cautionary tale.

Great book.

Writing

I have an entire laptop, several notebooks, and piled scraps of paper next to my bed, all full of crap I've written. Most of it is just terrible but I keep doing it anyway.

Some people ask me where I find the time to write, and the truth is, I don't know. That is, I didn't know until I read Mary Beth Danielson's article, "Seventeen Minutes of Kayaking," a few months ago.

In her essay Danielson talks about our need to honor our "inconvenient passions," to pursue what lights us up from the inside out, and to chase what is rightfully ours.

She suggests that spending a few hours writing every week actually made the rest of her life with toddlers and babies and commitments work. Reading her words made it dawn on me: writing helps me somehow fit the puzzle pieces of Jack and autism and family more neatly together. Because to write about my son I have to first really see him. And once I really see him, I want to write about him. I want to tell you about him.

So I make the time.

The Other Small People Who Live With Me

Whenever I am thoroughly confused by something Jack is saying or screaming or doing, I automatically look to Joey, Charlie, Rose, or Henry to help me out.

They are savvy, let me tell you. They are like little

Autism Whisperers. Over and over again they draw him out and pull him close, like the time we were all eating steamed clams with lots of butter and I really wanted Jack to try one. After a few minutes Joey advised, "Mom, you need to let him touch one first. He has to feel it before he will eat it."

Sure enough, once Jack cradled the clam shell in his palm and slid his finger around the edge, he popped a forkful into his mouth. "Huh. Slippery."

(Note: Ten-year-old Joey just read this part and suggested he's really a medium person, not a small person. So I suppose this particular "resource" should be titled "The Other Small *and Medium* People Who Live With Me.")

This Man

This is all I'll say about Joe:

Yes, some days I worry we won't make it, we won't last. But I know I could not breathe without him, and maybe that's enough.

He is my other perspective, my open window when the door is closed.

But he snores.

This Boy

Before Jack, I'd never known anyone who had autism. The only exposure I'd ever had with spectrum disorder came from *Rain Man*, the movie with Tom Cruise and Dustin Hoffman.

But now I live with someone who has autism. And every single day I learn from him.

When he was about three, it occurred to me that instead

of plopping him in front of one *Baby Einstein* video after another so I could scour the Internet to learn more about things like *joint attention* and *pervasive developmental disorder*, I would be better off watching and listening and hearing my own son.

Because, yes, Wikipedia told me that *joint attention* means "shared focus of two individuals on an object and is achieved when one individual alerts another to an object by means of eye-gazing, pointing or other verbal or non-verbal indications." But all I really needed to know was that when my neighbor walked his adorable little dog, Boots, past our window, and I pointed and said *look Jack there's Boots do you see?* Jack did not turn so much as a hair on his head to see what I was trying to show him.

Wikipedia never explained the way my stomach would lurch or the way I frantically started to point things out *bird dog tree cup mama dada look Jack look look look* like a crazy person.

Wikipedia didn't tell me that one day Jack *would* look. That he would follow my pointed finger to the bright blue sky and repeat *pwane sky pwane sky* as a giant airplane flew over our heads. And that I would feel simply weightless with joy, like I could have floated right up to the sky myself and bounced on a fluffy white cloud.

Wikipedia doesn't do that. Only Jack can.

I know, I know. Some list. Not even one website or support group or research article. But if parenting and autism has taught me anything, it's that I need to be whole so I can appreciate Jack's wholeness—his rare smile and his quick hugs and the way he organizes the K-cups into neat rows for my morning coffee.

I need to read and write and laugh and live out loud. I need to be brave, and I need to eat the brownie if I feel like eating the brownie.

Most of all, I need to chase what is rightfully mine, and some days that's nothing more than closing my eyes, taking a deep breath, and jumping the rope.

About the Author, In the Third Person

I was recently asked to write a bio about myself. This was harder than I expected.

You see, writers don't want to write about themselves, we'd much rather write about other people. Whenever a friend or my sister or Joe shares an amusing or embarrassing story about themselves, they usually say *do not write about this*. Unfortunately, all I hear is *definitely write about this it's so funny*. I mean, who wouldn't want to read about the time my husband bought me a butter dish shaped like a Buddha?

I asked my publisher what he thought I should write and to give me some examples of a typical author's biography. But he just encouraged me to write creatively so people can hear my voice and be sure to include all the blah-blah-blah stuff about birthplace and education and work experience and such. Oh, and to use the third person even though I'm talking about myself. Weird, right?

Well, here goes . . .

Carrie Cariello grew up in a teeny-tiny town in rural New York, a town called Wingdale. Wingdale was so small it had one stoplight. Back then she was Carrie Watterson, and always the tallest girl in her class.

After high school Carrie went on to get a Bachelor's of Science degree in Political Administration from the State University of New York, and then a Master's in Public Administration from Rockefeller College. During this time she met a dark-haired guy named Joe who wanted to become a dentist. On Easter Sunday in 1997, in her small apartment above a hair salon, he gave her a lovely sapphire ring and they laughed and cried and planned a wedding.

Together they moved to Buffalo, New York where he went to dental school and Carrie began a career in marketing. For ten years she worked for an extraordinary construction company called Lehigh Construction Group Inc., and she also got her MBA from Canisius College. She figured she might as well do something in the evenings while Joe was working in a dental lab making fake teeth.

While they were in Buffalo they had a son, Joey.

About a year later, they had another son, Jack. From the time he was a small baby wearing dark blue footie pajamas with snowflakes on them, Jack was different. He did not talk or babble or coo. He did not point. He did not have things like *joint attention* or *gross motor skills* or *eye contact*.

What he did have, Joe and Carrie eventually learned, was autism.

Some days and weeks and months were very hard with their son Jack. Some nights he barely slept and some days he barely smiled. Sometimes Carrie thought very mean, un-mom like things in her tired mind, things like *why can't you be normal* when he wouldn't wear his Halloween frog costume and *everyone is looking at us you are embarrassing me* when he threw loud ugly tantrums in the library. Some days she wished he was not so different.

They went on to have another boy and they named him Charlie. After Charlie was born in 2005 they moved to Bedford, New Hampshire, where they live today, after which followed two more children, Rose and Henry.

Carrie did not dream of becoming a writer as a little girl in Wingdale, New York. She did not have visions of tap-tap-tapping her life story on a laptop for people to read on Facebook or on a blog or in a book. But over time she learned she could best make sense of her long, frustrating days with Jack and his autism if she wrote about them. Over time, writing has helped her separate the boy from his diagnosis and discover that she fiercely loves them both. It has helped her make peace with her beautiful son. And like a prism with countless different angles and light and rainbows, sometimes she sees her own reflection in her writing. Sometimes she understands herself better.

There are days when she's writing and she thinks *this is a giant piece of crap why would anyone ever read this I am wasting my time.* But then she makes herself move forward to post, to publish, to reveal. And people seem to like it. People are following her. Because like that prism, people see their own reflections in her writing, they see tiny colorful bits of themselves and their families and their autistic children in her essays.

She gets her best ideas when she's driving her bright red minivan. Her kids call it the Red Hot Chili Pepper.

She and the dark-haired guy from college have been married for nearly fifteen years, and together they have four boys and one rosy daughter. Some days are long and difficult and exhausting while others are filled with color and music and chocolate-covered doughnuts. They are filled with laughter.

But no matter what kind of day it's been, whether one of tantrums and tears or lightness and bliss, there is always something to write about.

Acknowledgments

I'd like to thank the very first followers of my blog, Mary DeSenso from Pennsylvania and Dave Hofer in Buffalo.

When I first started writing posts every week, I would sit at my desk with my fingers on the keyboard and fight a rising panic. Would anyone even read it? Was it interesting? Do I use too many commas? Or not enough commas?

(Really, why are commas so hard?)

But I'd tell myself I just needed to write for Dave and Mary. I needed to write as if I was telling them a story or a joke, as if they could hear me all the way from New Hampshire. And so I did.

Thank you to Michael and Renee Charney, for the endless editing it takes to compile a bunch of posts into a cohesive book, for your patience during the cover design, and for always needing tissues when you read.

My deepest gratitude to all of the special teachers at Riddle Brook Elementary School; you showed a complicated boy how to add and subtract and spell and write, but most of all you showed him he belongs. For that, I thank you.

I'm deeply grateful to Joey, Charlie, Rose, and Henry for letting me share our story. You inspire me every single day with your laughter, your loyalty, and your love.

And thank you, Jack. For all the things you are and are not and will never be, for waffles on Thursdays and pancakes on Saturdays and the colors of the week that keep changing. You are my magical unicorn.

Most of all, thank you Joe, for letting me put our marriage and our life on display, for your patience and support, and for always, always having something more to give. MYITM

I CAN!
JACK

CPSIA information can be obtained
at www.ICGtesting.com
Printed in the USA
LVOW10s2004260917
550186LV00001B/35/P